Wyom Estate Exam Prep:

The Complete Guide to Passing the Wyoming AMP Real Estate Salesperson License Exam the First Time!

Laura Miller

Published by Createspace, Charleston, SC

Printed in the United States of America

ISBN: 978-1986326995

This book is for educational purposes only. It is presented on an "as is" basis as a supplemental study tool and is not intended to substitute for any educational course or textbook.

The use of this guide does not guarantee that anyone will qualify for, or pass, any particular exam. Sample questions in this guide cover subject areas that may be included in real estate exams and are not represented as actual questions appearing on any exam.

Table of Contents

Introduction

Your Ticket to Passing the Wyoming Real Estate Licensing Exam!

If you are concerned about passing the Wyoming Real Estate Licensing Exam, then this book is for you.

This book explains key concepts that you need to know. It was written as a concise and easy-to-use guide to help you ace your Wyoming Licensing Exam on the first try!

About the Book:

Wyoming Real Estate Exam Prep: The Complete Guide to Passing the Wyoming AMP Real Estate Salesperson License Exam the First Time includes:

- **Test taking tips & strategies;**
- **A comprehensive real estate review;**
- **A comprehensive math review;**
- **A full glossary of real estate terms;**
- **Flashcards; and,**
- **Four practice tests with answers and explanations.**

Chapter 1

Test-Taking Tips

About the Test

The State of Wyoming has retained the services of AMP, a PSI business, to develop and administer their real estate examination program. As a full-service testing company, PSI/AMP provides expertise and support to associations, state credentialing agencies and private industry in examination development, scoring and reporting of examinations.

The exam is administered on an electronic testing system. The testing system eliminates the use of paper, pencil and answer sheets.

The Wyoming Real Estate Salesperson Examination is comprised of two separate portions, the national portion which is 100 questions and the state-specific portion which is 32 questions. The total time allowed for both portions of the examination is 3 ½ hours. The questions on the two portions will be intermixed and will not appear as separate sections.

After you have completed the Salesperson examination, you will be instructed to report to the testing supervisor to receive your score report. Your score report will show your result for your examination and will give diagnostic scoring information for any portion you did not pass. To be eligible to apply for a salesperson license in Wyoming, you must pass both the National and State examination.

The passing score for the national examination is 70 correct answers, and the passing score for the state examination is 24 correct answers.

In the event., you don't pass the entire exam or one of the sections, you will need to retake this examination by scheduling another appointment through PSI's Candidate Services.

Once you have successfully completed and passed your 54 hour Salesperson licensing at your real estate school and passed their test you may register to take the test at https://goamp.com.

Test-Taking Tips

Since it may have been sometime since you have last taken a test, I thought that I would take the time to go through some test-taking tips and techniques that will help you when it does come time to sit and take your test. These tips will help you to be calm, cool and collected when it comes time for you to sit t for your test and may even add as much as 10 to 15 points to your score.

- **Make flashcards.**

We would like for you to prepare flashcards as you go along. In addition to a comprehensive Glossary, we have created a Flashcards chapter section that you can use to get started. The more cards, the better. Have fun with it.

- **Be confident.**

When taking your test, I want you to be confident. Don't underestimate yourself. You have studied and prepared. With a confident mindset you can go in there and tackle the test without a problem. Remember you can get over twenty questions wrong on this test and still pass.

- **Keep it to yourself.**

Please don't tell people you are taking the test. By telling your family, friends and colleagues that you are taking a test creates undue pressure on yourself. You are taking the test for you. You don't want to worry about your mother or father's expectations of you. You want all the pressure off of you so that you can comfortably and confidently complete the test. Tell people that you have postponed taking the test for a bit and then actually take the test.

- **Know the rules.**

Test moderators enforce the regulations closely. When you schedule your test, you will be given specific requirements about what you can bring into the testing room and what you cannot bring. Pay attention to the guidelines and follow them closely. Don't fail your test because of a simple technicality. Make sure to be early and make sure that you don't bring your smartphone to use as your calculator. Make sure that you bring a proper calculator.

- **Don't cram.**

Your course has covered a sweeping amount of material. It is best to learn gradually so the information sticks with you. Cramming for a test of this breadth and scope will get you nowhere. Instead, take some practice exams, bone up on your vocabulary, make some flashcards and know the concepts. A proper night's rest and a decent meal will help you ace the test.

- **Answer questions that you know first then go back to the other questions.**

Do not spend a lot of time on one question. Go through the test answering only those questions you know are correct. If you're in doubt, skip the question and go to the next one. It's best to move through the questions you can answer as quickly as possible and return to the others later, if you have time. If you are in doubt about a question, skip it, and move on. Once you have moved through the entire test answering the questions you know, go back and review all marked questions. Sometimes, other questions in the test will help you answer a question you are unsure of.

- **Look for the best answer.**

If a question on the test appears to have more than one correct answer, look for the best answer based on the supplied information—not your assumptions. Take your time and reason through the question. If you jump to assumptions that aren't there, you will miss the question. There will always be one choice that is the best answer.

- **Breathe, relax and keep calm.**

Maintain your concentration. You may lose your train of thought because a question appears to be poorly written, makes no sense, or has more than one correct answer. Getting caught on one of these can throw you off for a series of questions to follow. When this happens, relax your mind and your muscles—and skip the question. There may be three or four of these questions on the test. If, by chance, you miss them because you had to guess, you will not fail. What causes you to fail the test is becoming so frustrated that you miss the second, third, or fourth question after that.

Keep your composure. Remember, even if you miss these and no others, you will still pass.

- **Take your time and read the question completely.**

Make sure to read the questions carefully. There is plenty of time for this multiple-choice test. Think of the test as a marathon rather than a sprint. Take your time. Read the question and answers slowly and carefully.

When reading a question, do not jump to a quick conclusion. Before you choose an answer, be sure you have read the entire question and all answer choices. It's very easy to miss a critical word if you read too quickly.

- **Get a good night's rest and eat a healthy meal.**

Make sure to be well rested and get a healthy meal in you before the test. This will ensure that your mind is sharp and ready to ace the test.

Chapter 2

Real Estate Review

Wyoming Statutes (Title 33: Chapter 28). Licensee

Wyoming Statutes Title 33, Chapter 28 forms part of the Wyoming Property Law. The name that it has been given is "Wyoming Real Estate License Law". It sets forth your rights and obligations as a Licensee. A Licensee is either a broker or a salesperson who holds a Wyoming Real Estate License.

Types of Property

There are two main categories of property that are discussed in real estate. These are personal and real property.

Personal property refers to property that is tangible and movable. Examples of tangible property would be lamps, cabinets, plants that have been superficially planted and furniture. Personal property does not include many rights to the land. Sometimes, however, personal property also known as chattel becomes real property if it later becomes a permanent fixture. For example, the timber that is used in the construction of a house moves from the distinction of personal property to real property.

Real property refers to land and items that are permanently attached to it such as plants, minerals and the buildings on the land. The home that you live in and the trees that surround your home would be considered real property.

Generally, real property plus the bundle of rights is 'Real Estate'.

Physical & Economic Characteristics of Land

The three physical characteristics of land are:

- **Immobility;**
- **Indestructibility; and,**
- **non-homogeneity (uniqueness).**

Immobility

Land is physically immobile and cannot be moved from one location to another. Although you may remove something may be removed or replaced, the original part of the land remains and will continue to grow.

Indestructibility

Land cannot be destroyed. Its value may be destroyed by changing conditions but physically land goes on forever.

Non-homogeneity

Land and improvements are not standardized or homogeneous. Every property is unique. In other words, no two pieces of land are alike.

The four economic characteristics of land:

Scarcity: Land is considered to be a scarce resource that is not limitless There is a limited supply of land. The concept derives from the fact that land is fixed and can never be increased.

Improvements: Improvements are part of the parcel so to speak and are normally value-added for that particular piece of real estate.

Permanence: AKA Fixity refers to the long-term stability associated with real estate. If you put a house on your property you expect it to be there forever.

Situs: Area preference that consist of two factors:

1. certain locations are more preferable than others (location, location, location)
2. real estate is immobile

Property Descriptions:

The main legal descriptions used in Wyoming are:

1) **Metes and Bounds** – A method of describing real property that uses geography and land features with directions and distances to describe the boundaries of land. The starting point in a survey of this type is the Point of Origin.

2) **Recorded Plat** – aka the lot and block survey system; this system is used for lots in a variety of areas such as heavily populated metropolitan, suburban, and exurbs. This is used to plot large areas of a property into smaller lots and land areas.

3) **Monument** - Method this sometime is used instead of metes and bounds. Surveyors use monument when they are describing large areas of land that may be cost prohibitive to survey.

4) **Rectangular Survey System** – Traditional method of surveying property and it measures factors such as the precise length of the line run, natural materials (flora/ fauna) and surface and land soil.

5) **Government or US Public Land Survey System (PLSS)** – Most commonly used method to survey and spatially identify land or property parcels before designating ownership, whether for sale or transfer.

6) **Townships** – A survey method that refers to square units of land that is six miles on each side. Townships exist at the intersection of range and tier. Each 36-Square-Mile Township is divided into 36 one-square mile sections that can be further sub-divided for sale.

7) **Principal Meridians** – Method that uses principal meridian lines for survey control in a large region that divides the townships by North/ South/ East/ West. The meridian meets its corresponding

initial point for land survey. Base lines and meridians mark land into tiers every six miles.

8) **Base Line and Meridian Intersections** – Base lines run horizontally (East to West) and meridians run vertically (North to South). Base lines and meridians mark land into tiers every six miles.

9) **Assessor's Parcel Number (APN)** – Also known as an appraisal's account number, a number assigned to parcels of property by the area's jurisdiction for identification and record keeping. Each APN is unique within the particular jurisdiction and should conform to certain formatting standards that hold identifying information such as property type or location within a Plat Map.

Licensing Requirements in Wyoming

An individual is eligible for a salesperson's license if she:

- is at least 18 years of age;
- fulfills a 54-hour qualifying course;
- successfully passes the exam; and,
- obtains broker sponsorship.

If an applicant has ever been convicted of a crime or is currently on parole or probation their application for a real estate license may be denied.

All real estate licenses are valid for three years.

Renewal/Continuing Education:

In order to be eligible for renewal or reinstatement of a real estate license, every individual licensed as a broker, broker-salesperson or salesperson must complete 45 hours of continuing education every three-year cycle.

There are a host of activities in real estate that require a license when a fee is charged. These are:

- Sales
- Exchanges
- Purchases
- Rentals/ Leases
- Negotiating
- Offers
- Listings
- Options
- Advertising Real Property
- Loan negotiating
- Apartment searching

Persons that do not require a real estate license:

- Attorneys who have passed the WY State Bar Exam
- Public Officers in performance of official duties
- Individuals under the judgement or order of the court

- Tenant Associations and Nonprofit Organizations
- Building Superintendents and maintenance personnel

Agency Law

When one person is hired to act on behalf of another person, an agency relationship is created.

The person hired on the other person's behalf is the agent.

· An agency relationship is consensual.

· The person who selects the agent to act on his behalf is the principal or client.

· The Customer of an agent is the party whom the agent brings to the principal as a seller or buyer of the property.

An agent is one who represents the fiduciary interest of his client. There are two types of agencies: single and dual. In a dual agency the agent represents both buyer and seller. In the state of Wyoming this type of agency is allowed with informed consent and disclosure.

6 Fiduciary Duties of a Real Estate Agent

The relationship between a real estate agent and a client is called a *fiduciary relationship*. *Fiduciary* means faithful servant, and an agent is a fiduciary of the client. In real estate, a broker or a salesperson can be the agent of a seller or a buyer.

Here's a list of the fiduciary duties that an agent owes her client:

- **Accounting:** The agent must account for all funds entrusted to her and not *commingle* (combine) client/customer funds with her personal and/or business funds.

- **Reasonable Care:** The agent must use all of her skills to the best of her ability on behalf of the client.

- **Confidentiality:** The agent must keep confidential any information given to her by her client, especially information that may be damaging to the client in a negotiation.

- **Disclosure:** The agent must disclose to the client any information she receives that may benefit the client's position in a negotiation.

- **Loyalty:** The agent owes undivided loyalty to the client and puts the client's interests above her own.

- **Obedience:** The agent must obey all lawful orders that the client gives her.

In general, people use the **anacronym OLDCAR** to remember these fiduciary duties.

4 Types of Listing Agreements for Real Estate Agents

- **Exclusive right to sell listing:** In this agreement, the agent gets paid no matter who sells the property, regardless of whether it's the agent or the seller.

- **Exclusive agency listing:** Agents get paid in this type of agreement only if they sell the property. No fee is earned if the owner alone sells the property.

- **Open listing:** In this type of agreement, sellers have the right to use as many brokers as they want. However, the seller isn't obligated to pay any of them if he or she sells the property without the broker's help.

- **Net listing:** This type of agreement is illegal in Wyoming. The agent gets to keep everything he can get that's more than the sale price the owner wants.

Real Estate Settlement Procedures Act of 1974 - RESPA

This act was designed to protect potential homeowners and enable them to become more intelligent consumers. RESPA requires that lenders provide greater amounts of information to prospective borrowers at certain points in the loan settlement process. It also prohibits the various parties involved from paying kickbacks to each other.

4 Kinds of Real Estate Ownership

There are several types of property ownership, and you need to know about them to pass the real estate license exam.

Here are the four most common types of property ownership:

- **Tenancy in severalty:** Although it may sound like more, this type of ownership is by one person or a corporation.

- **Tenancy in common:** Equal or unequal undivided ownership between two or more people is what characterizes this type of ownership. If an owner dies, the deceased person's share is conveyed to his or her heirs, not the other owners.

- **Joint tenancy:**

The four unities that must exist for this type of ownership to exist are:

  - **Interest:** Each owner has the same interest.

  - **Possession:** All owners hold an undivided interest.

  - **Time:** All owners receive their interest at the same time.

  - **Title:** All owners acquire their interest with the same deed.

If one owner of a joint tenancy dies, that owner's interest reverts to the other owners. This right of survivorship may vary by state.

- **Tenancy by the entirety:** Ownership that's available only to married couples, tenancy by the entirety means that property may not be sold without the agreement of both parties. The right of survivorship exists to the extent that if one spouse dies, his/her interest reverts to the other spouse.

Bundle of Rights

The Bundle of Rights are the rights that go along with owning real estate. These rights are:

- **Possession (Access and Use)**

- **Quiet Enjoyment (No Noise, Nuisance, etc.)**

- **Disposal (Sell, Give Away, etc.)**

- **Exclusion (Keep People Out)**

- **Control (Build, Tear Down, Lease, Farm, Mine, etc.)**

If you own **fee simple**, you possess all of the rights. If you rent or own a lessor estate you have some of the rights. Renters, for example, maintain the rights of possession, quiet enjoyment and exclusion, but certainly not control or disposition.

A quick memory device to remember these is: "mind your **P's** and **Q's** or I will **DEC** you!"

Water Rights

Water rights are one of the interests that may attach to real estate ownership, and pertain to the rights to use adjacent bodies of water. These are:

1) **Riparian rights** are awarded to land owners whose property is located along a river, stream or lake. Typically, landowners have the right to use the water as long as such use does not harm upstream or downstream neighbors. In the event, the water is a non-navigable waterway the landowner generally owns the land beneath the water to the exact center of the waterway.

2) **Littoral rights** pertain to landowners whose land border large, navigable lakes and oceans. Landowners with littoral rights have unrestricted access to the waters but own the land only to the median high-water mark. After this point, the land is owned by the government.

Water rights are appurtenant, meaning they are attached to the land and not to the owner. In other words, if an ocean front property is sold, the new owner gains the littoral rights; the seller relinquishes his or her rights.

If a question were to come up on the test regarding water rights, just remember that Riparian is for River and Littoral is for lake.

Encumbrances

An ENCUMBRANCE is defined as anything which affects or limits the fee simple title to or value of property, e.g., mortgages or easements. Some types of encumbrances are:

- **ENCROACHMENT** — An unlawful intrusion onto another's adjacent property by improvements to real property, e.g. a swimming pool built across a property line.

- **EASEMENT** — A right, privilege or interest limited to a specific purpose which one party has in the land of another.

  o **Easement Appurtenant:** Typically benefits the land and is transferred automatically if the property is transferred to another party. It is said to: "run with the land".

  o **Easement in Gross:** Typically benefits the individual or legal party and can be used for personal or commercial use. While this type of easement is not inherited or assignable, it can be transferred for business purposes.

- **LIEN** — A form of encumbrance which usually makes specific property security for the payment of a debt or discharge of an obligation. Example — judgments, taxes, mortgages, deeds of trust, etc.

  o **Mechanic's lien:** A lien that exists for real and personal property and initiated by those who have supplied labor or materials to improve the property (carpenters, landscapers).

  o **Material Man's lien**: similar to the mechanic's lien, but applies more to the person or company that supplies the materials being used.

- **FORECLOSURE** — Procedure whereby property pledged as security for a debt is sold to pay the debt in event of default in payments or terms.

- **JUDGMENT** — The final determination of a court of competent jurisdiction of a matter presented to it; money judgments provide for the payment of claims presented to the court, or are awarded as damages, etc.

- o **Writ of attachment:** a court order to seize an asset.

- o **Writ of execution:** written in order to force a judgement made against an asset, usually to collect an asset that has been ordered to be turned over.

- **Tax liens** – a type of lien obtained on the property, including all land right, imposed by the government's taxing authority, often used for payment of federal taxes.

  - o **Property tax lien:** a lien to seize the assets on a property or set of properties.

  - o **Federal tax lien:** a lien to seize federal taxes that have not been paid.

  - o **State tax lien:** a lien to seize state taxes that have not been paid.

Liens can be considered **voluntary** or **involuntary**. For example, a homeowner voluntarily takes a mortgage out on his or her house, but in the case of back taxes the government can involuntarily place a lien on your property.

Types of Tenancies

Tenancy for years or fixed-term tenancy

A fixed-term tenancy or tenancy for years lasts for some fixed period of time. It has a definite beginning date and a definite ending date. Despite the name "tenancy for years", such a tenancy can last for any period of time—even a tenancy for one week may be called a tenancy for years. A fixed term tenancy comes to an end automatically when the fixed term runs out.

Periodic tenancy

A periodic tenancy, also known as a tenancy from year to year, month to month, or week to week, is an estate that exists for some period of time determined by the term of the payment of rent

Tenancy at will

A *tenancy at will* is a tenancy which either the landlord or the tenant may terminate at any time by giving reasonable notice. Unlike a periodic tenancy, it isn't associated with a time period. It may last for many years, but it could be ended at any time by either the lessor or the lessee for any reason, or for no reason at all. Proper notice, as always with landlord/tenant law, must be given, as set forth in the state's statutes. If there is no formal lease, the tenancy at will is the one that usually exists.

Tenancy at sufferance

A *tenancy at sufferance* (sometimes called a *holdover tenancy*) exists when a tenant remains in possession of a property after the expiration of a lease, and until the landlord acts to eject the tenant from the property. At this point, the tenant is technically a trespasser.

Leases

A **lease** is a contract outlining the terms under which one party agrees to rent property owned by another party. Leases or enforceable when both the landlord and tenant sign.

Gross Lease

A gross lease is a type of commercial lease where the landlord pays for the building's property taxes, insurance and maintenance. A gross lease can be modified to meet the needs of a particular building's tenants. For example, a gross lease may require the tenant to pay the utility bills. An example, would be an apartment lease.

Net Lease

A provision that requires the tenant to pay a portion or all of the taxes, fees and maintenance costs for the property in addition to rent. Net lease requirements are most commonly used with commercial real estate. There are three primary types of net leases: single (net), double (net-net) and triple (net-net-net).

Single Net Lease

Single net lease (Net), the lessee or tenant is responsible for paying property taxes.

Double Net Lease

In a double net lease (Net-Net), the lessee or tenant is responsible for property tax and building insurance. The lessor or landlord is responsible for any expenses incurred for structural repairs and common area maintenance.

Triple Net Lease

A triple net lease (triple-Net) is a lease agreement on a property where the tenant or lessee agrees to pay all real estate taxes, building insurance, and maintenance (the three "nets") on the property in addition to any normal fees that are expected under the agreement (rent, utilities, etc.). In such a lease, the tenant or lessee is responsible for all costs associated with the repair and maintenance of any common area. Common Area Maintenance (CAM) fees typically are negotiated up front as a set dollar figure per square foot. This form of lease is most frequently used for commercial freestanding buildings. However, it has also been used in single-family residential rental real estate properties.

Percentage Lease

A percentage lease is a lease where the rental is based on a percentage of the monthly or annual gross sales made on the premises, usually coupled with a base rent. This is usually used in shopping centers and malls.

Graduated Lease

 A type of long-term, typically for commercial property, lease in which the payments are variable and adjusted periodically to reflect changes in the property's appraised value or changes in a certain publicized benchmark rate, such as the Consumer Price Index (CPI).

Ground Lease

A ground lease is a long-term agreement (50-99 years) in which a tenant is permitted to develop a piece of property during the lease period, after which the land and all improvements are turned over to the property owner. A ground lease indicates that the improvements will be owned by the property owner unless an exception is created, and stipulates that all relevant taxes incurred during the lease period will be paid by the tenant.

Federal Environmental Laws

The Federal Government has many environmental laws. For this review, you only have to know these which all came about in the 1970s:

- **The Clean Air Act;**
- **The Clean Water Act;**
- **The Safe Drinking Water Act; and,**
- **CERCLA/ Superfund (Comprehensive, Response, Compensation and Liability Act).**

The Clean Air Act: The enactment of the **Clean Air Act of 1970 (1970 CAA)** resulted in a major shift in the federal government's role in air pollution control. This legislation authorized the development of comprehensive federal and state regulations to limit emissions from both stationary (industrial) sources and mobile sources.

The Clean Water Act: As reorganized and expanded in 1972, the law became commonly known as the **Clean Water Act(CWA)**. The 1972 amendments: Established the basic structure for regulating pollutant discharges into the waters of the United States. Gave EPA the authority to implement pollution control programs such as setting wastewater standards for industry.

The Safe Drinking Water Act: The **Safe Drinking Water Act (SDWA)**, which was originally enacted into law in 1974, focuses on ensuring that public drinking water meets appropriate safety standards; in contrast, the Clean Water Act regulates pollution in our nation's lakes, rivers, and other bodies of water.

CERCLA/ Superfund (Comprehensive, Response, Compensation and Liability Act): **CERCLA** stands for the Comprehensive Environmental Response, Compensation, and Liability Act, known also as Superfund. It was passed in 1980 in response to some alarming and decidedly unacceptable hazardous waste practices and management going on in the 1970s.

Lead Paint Law/ Lead Disclosure Guidelines

In 1996 HUD and the Environmental Protection Agency, known as EPA, set guidelines for lead based paint disclosure. This disclosure obligation was put into print September,1996. It was put in place to protect the public and covers homes that were built prior to 1978. Federal law requires that individuals must receive this information prior to renting or buying or when renovations are being done.

Landlords are required to disclose known lead based paint conditions to their prospective tenants. A federal form must be included and attached to the lease. Also, the EPA pamphlet Protect Your Family from Lead in Your Home must be distributed.

Sellers would have to disclose known lead based paint to a prospective buyer and the completed disclosure form would be attached to the sales contract. The buyer is entitled to receive a 10 point risk assessment as to whether or not the home has lead. The EPA pamphlet Protect Your Family from Lead in Your Home will be distributed.

Renovators who disturb more than 2 square feet must present the pamphlet as well before starting any renovations. It is always recommended that when a contractor is renovating your home a lead test be done to determine if lead is present. Young children and pregnant adults should be removed from the home during the renovation process

Condominiums (Condos) Co-operatives (Co-ops) and Condops

A **condominium** is a complex in which the residents own their respective units and a percentage of the common areas (lobby, stairs, pools, basement, parking, etc.) as a tenant in common with the other residents. A condominium owner gets a deed and a mortgage.

A **co-operative (co-op)** is when a corporation owns an a complex. People who wish to live in the complex buy shares in the corporation and own part of the complex indirectly. Therefore, a co-op owner gets a stock certificate and a proprietary lease.

A **condominium** is real property owned in freehold and a co-op is considered personal property possessed in leasehold, as the owner doesn't physically own their apartment. The co-op's Board of Directors is responsible for running the co-operative corporation, although they usually hire a property manager for this.

In a **condominium**, owners pay real estate tax and common charges for maintenance of the common areas of the complex like cleaning, the pool, the lobby, repairs, snow removal, etc.

In **a co-op**, shareholders pay monthly maintenance, which also covers the common areas. Moreover, it pays for a portion or the building's mortgage and real estate tax. Mortgage interest and real estate tax are tax deductible, therefore part of your maintenance is tax deductible on your income tax.

Condop

A **condop** is a building that is part condominium and co-op. Just think of a building where you have a doctor's office at the bottom that is owned as a condo. Then, the remainder of the building upstairs is owned as a corporation where the units become co-ops.

Multiple Listing Service (MLS): a shared system among participating member brokerages with respect to real estate property for sale.

Fair Housing and Consumer Protection Laws

Federal Civil Rights Act of 1866 – with respect to home sellers and real estate brokerages, they are not allowed to discriminate racially against anyone in the process of selling, leasing or any other activity regarding real or personal property.

Federal Fair Housing Act of 1968 (Title VII): prevents the discrimination of individuals based on race, sex, color, religion, national origin, handicap, and familial status with respect to sale or renting of housing or land. For example, some actions that are prohibited:

- Not selling or renting to someone based on protected classes. Protected classes are color, race, religion, national origin, handicap or family status.
- **Redlining:** An illegal lending policy of denying real estate loans on properties in older, changing urban areas, usually with large minority populations, because of alleged higher lending risks without due consideration being given by the lending institution to the credit worthiness of the individual loan applicant.
- **Blockbusting:** The practice on the part of unscrupulous speculators or real estate agents of inducing panic selling of homes at prices below market value, especially by exploiting the prejudices of property owners in neighborhoods in which the racial make-up is changing or appears to be on the verge of changing.
- **Steering:** Encouraging individuals towards or away from a specific neighborhood based on a protected class such as race.
- Dishonestly telling that a property in unavailable for rent or sale when it is.

Sherman Antitrust Act of 1890

Passed in 1890, the **Sherman Antitrust Act** was the first major legislation passed to address oppressive business practices associated with cartels and oppressive monopolies. It ensures free competition in real estate. Here are some of what it prohibits:

- Price fixing;
- Real estate companies controlling one particular geographical area;
- Real estate companies from knowing directing business away from their competition; and,
- Brokers from having unfair access to marketing and sales information.

Know the Difference Between Mortgagee vs Mortgagor

Since the buyer/borrower is pledging the property, he/she is "mortgaging" the property and in known as the **"mortgagor"**. The lender is the recipient of the pledge, and therefore is the **"mortgagee"**. Just remember: The mortgagor mortgages the property to the mortgagee.

Chapter 3

Math Review

In this chapter, we are going to quickly cover real estate math and what you should expect on the test and in your future.

The good news is that the math is relatively straight-forward and doable and that there aren't that many on the test. You should really try to think of these as easy points to gather to pass your exam.

Some of the math question types that you may come across on your exam include:

- **Area**
- **Perimeter**
- **Percent**
- **Commissions**
- **Proration**
- **Proceeds from sales**
- **Depreciation**
- **Return on Investment (ROI)**
- **And more**

Linear Measurements

12 inches	1 foot
3 feet	1 yard
16 ½ feet	1 pole
5,280	1 Mile, 80 chains

Cubic Measurement

27 cubic feet	1 cubic yard
1 cubic foot	7.48 gallons

Square Measurement

43,560 square feet	1 acre, 10 square chains
2.47 acres	1 hectare (10,000 square meters)
640 acres	1 square mile
1 square mile	1 section
36 sections	1 township
9 square feet	1 square yard

Front Feet

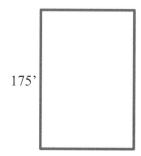

175'

100'

Frontage or front feet is the portion of the lot that faces the street. In a measurement the front feet is always the first number. In this example, the lot is 100'x 175'. Therefore, the frontage is 100 feet.

Perimeter Measurement

To find the perimeter of a lot you would simply add up all the sides of the lot.

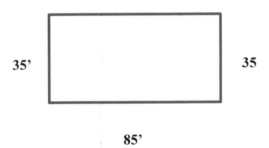

Therefore, for example, if on the test they asked you to find out how many feet of fencing a lot required, you would add together the sides.

35'+ 85'+ 35'+ 85'=240 feet.

The above lot would require 240 linear feet of fencing.

Area Measurement:

To determine the area of a rectangle or square that the formula is:

Area = Width x Length (AWL)

Area ÷ Width = Length

Area ÷ Length = Width

Therefore, if given a rectangle with the following measurements

135'
135' x 265' = 35,775 SQ FT

265'

You would arrive at 35,775 SQ FT.

To this end, if you were given the Area and the Width you would be able to calculate the Length as follows:

If given the area and length and asked to find the width, for example, divide the area by the length:

33,750 Square Feet ÷ 135 Feet (Width) = 256 Feet (Length)

Area of a Triangular Shaped Lot

Sometimes you are going to find triangular shaped lots.

The typical formula for this is Area=1/2 bh

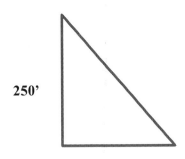

250'

150'

If you are presented with this simply plug the base and height into the formula

A=1/2 bh

A=1/2 (250*150)

A= ½ (37,500 SQ. FT)

A=18,750 SQ.FT

Cubic Measurement

Cubic measurement is usually called on when determining the space in a room or the volume in a pool.

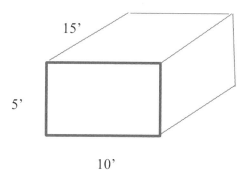

Length X Width X Height = Volume

For example:
A pool is 15' long, 10' wide, and 5' deep. The volume of the pool is:

15'x 10' x 5' = 750 Cubic Feet

To convert cubic feet to cubic yards, it's necessary to divide by 27 (3x3x3):
750 Cubic Feet ÷ 27 = 27.77 Cubic Yards

Irregular Areas

Lots, and for that matter floor plans never come in a standard cookie cutter one size fits all, but rather many different shapes and sizes. Normally, to find the acreage of a lot or the square feet in a floor plan you can take the various shapes within a floor plan or the lot and then simply add them all up.

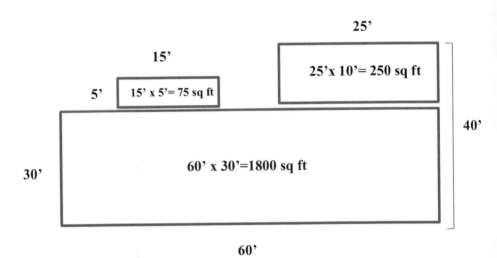

In this example, 75 + 250 + 1800 =2125 square feet.

T-Math

Many real estate situations require the ability to calculate percentages, for example, commissions or property assessments. An easy method for solving these problems is called T-math. When using T-math, the horizontal line means divide and the vertical line means multiply.

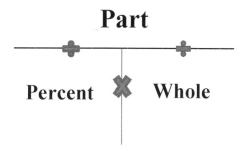

When calculating percentages, the part goes on the top of the T. The percent goes on the bottom, and the whole goes on the bottom opposite the percent.

When you know any two variables, you can easily find the third:

Percent x Whole = Part
Part ÷ Percent = Whole
Part ÷ Whole = Percent

Commission

When working with commission, the commission is the part, the commission rate is the percent, and the sale price is the whole:

Sale Price x Rate = Commission
Commission ÷ Rate = Sale Price
Commission ÷ Sale Price = Rate

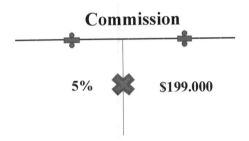

Fern Hallow Realty, for example, sells one of its properties for $199,000. If the commission is 5% what would be the total commission? This rate would be found simply by multiplying the percentage by the whole.

.05 x $199,000 = $9950. Therefore, the total commission would be $9950.

Net to Seller

Proceeds from sales or net to seller is an estimate of what a seller should receive from a sale after all expenses associated with the transaction have been paid. This is important information when considering both a listing price for the property and deciding whether to accept an offer.

For example, Alan wants to sell his home. He must pay off his existing $29,000 mortgage and pay $3,100 in closing costs. He wants to have

$35,000 left so he can buy another home. If he pays a 5% commission, what is the minimum offer he can accept?

First, subtract the known commission rate from the total sale price to find the percentage of the sale the seller will net:

100% - 5% = 95%

Total up the other known expenses:

$29,000 + $3,100 + $35,000 = $67,100

Finally, divide the total expenses by the net to seller percent:

$67,100 ÷ 0.95 = $70,631.58

Alan must sell his house for a minimum of $70,631.58.

Principal and Interest

Interest is the cost of borrowing money, while principal is the balance of the loan. The T-math strategy can be used to solve problems involving interest. The annual interest is the part, so it goes on the top. The principal is the whole, so it goes on the bottom with the interest rate. If you know any two factors in the equation, you can easily find the third.

Annual Interest

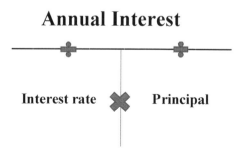

Interest rate ✖ Principal

For example, if the loan balance (principal) is $129,000 and the interest rate is 6.5%, the annual interest would be:

.065 x $129,000 = $8,385

That number, divided by 12, indicates the monthly interest on the loan balance. If the borrower makes a monthly mortgage payment of $850, it's possible to see how much of that payment is applied to the principal that month:

$8,385 ÷ 12 = $698.75 Monthly Interest
$850 - $698.75 = $141.25 Applied to Principal

Return on Investment (ROI)

If you know the original purchase price of a house and then the later sale price of the house, it is possible to determine the Return on Investment (ROI) also termed the percent of profit. In the event, the seller took a loss it would be termed the percent of loss.

Profit/ Original Purchase Price = Percentage of Profit or

Loss / Original Purchase Price = Percentage of Loss

For example, a house is purchased and $150,000 and later sold at $199,000

The profit is $49,000. Therefore, $49,000/$150,000 = .3266 or 32.66% Profit

Chapter 4

Flashcards

In this chapter, I want you to cover up the answers in the right column with your hand or index card and work your way through the questions. Once you have done that, I would like for you to start your own series of Flashcards. These should make a nice start but do try to add more to help aid in your studies.

Questions:	Answers:
Zoning board of appeals issues what kind of permits?	Variances and special use permits.
Who licenses mortgage brokers?	The license is issued by the Department of Finance.
Who can obtain a VA loan?	Veterans or spouses of deceased veterans.
When selling a house in WY is it necessary to disclose that there is a utility charge?	Yes
When salesperson Kate James left Hudson Realty to work with Fern Hallow Realty. What happens to her listings?	Remained with Jackson Realty.
When is registration with the Banking Department Necessary?	To negotiate a mortgage loan on residential property (one to four family building).

When is a deed valid?	Once its delivered and accepted.
What kind of lease allows the lessee to pay for all or some of the expenses of a property?	Net lease
What is Usury?	Charging more than the legal interest rate.
What is the civil rights act of 1866?	Prohibits any type of discrimination based on race.
What are blind ads?	When the real estate broker fails to indicate that they are brokers.
What happens if I do not renew my license?	You cannot conduct any real estate activities that require a Wyoming State real estate license.
Violation of the license law is a misdemeanor with a fine up to?	$1,000
Under the General Obligations Law, where must security deposits paid by a tenant be held?	Escrow account
To create an agency relationship, it is necessary that...	The parties act as principal and agent.
The type of mortgage loan that has an interest rate that may increase or decrease at different times in accordance to an economic indicator.	ARM (Adjustable Rate Mortgage)
The type of listing illegal in Wyoming is?	Net listing
The right of a government or its agent to expropriate private property for public use, with payment of compensation.	Eminent domain
The practice of denying or charging more for a loan in certain locations.	Redlining
The listing salesperson must accept compensation directly from the...	Employing broker

The Jacksons sold their house to the Andersons and are to close on August 1. The Jacksons paid their annual town taxes in January. At the closing, the Andersons will reimburse the Jacksons for...	The tax for the balance of the year.
The document used to convey title legally to real property	Deed
The borrower in a mortgage?	Mortgagor
The act of either: replacing an obligation to perform with a new obligation; or; adding an obligation to perform or replacing a party to an agreement with a new party.	Novation
Sky Realty is worried that its Commission on a sale will not be paid. Sky realty may...	File an affidavit of entitlement.
RESPA prohibits the payment of?	Kickbacks
Land use is regulated by?	Subdivision regulations
John is a broker and he accepts a $4,000 deposit. What should he do with it?	Place it in his escrow account immediately.
John Banks gave Star Realty an exclusive agency listing on her property. If he sells the Property himself without involving Star Realty, he will owe Star Realty how much?	No commission
Is the Department of Veterans Affairs mortgage a guaranteed loan program?	Yes
Is a salesperson that is also an independent contractor paid commission based on sales results?	Yes
Is a real estate license needed in WY to sell land at an auction?	Yes
Is a net listing legal in Wyoming?	No
Is a "barn" considered chattel?	No
Insures loans protect lenders against financial loss.	FHA

In order for a licensee to become partners at a real estate firm, what license must he or she have?	Broker's license
In a buyer/agency relationship, the broker owes the seller...	Fair and honest dealing.
If your license is revoked, how long must you wait before applying to have the license reinstated?	1 Year
If you purchase land or property on a stream, then you have rights to the stream known as?	Riparian rights
If asbestos is in area that is not disturbed is it sometimes best to leave it alone?	Yes
If a real estate broker earned a commission of $6,000 at a commission rate of 6%, at what price was the property sold?	$100,000
If a property lies in an agricultural district, is the licensee required to disclose such information to a potential buyer?	Yes
If a lessee transfers all the remaining interest of his lease to another party, who then must pay the owner is called an...?	Assignment
Highest form of legal estate in freehold land denoting complete ownership	Fee simple
Guiding prospective home buyers towards or away from certain neighborhoods based on their race.	Racial steering
Electrical systems are routed through a...	Circuit box
Does a real estate management company need a real estate broker's license?	If you collect rent or place tenants in vacant spaces on behalf of your landlord client, the answer is yes.
Does a new construction need a certificate of occupancy when the building permit has already issued?	Yes

Deed restrictions could only be established by the "Grantor". (T/F)	TRUE
Contractual arrangement calling for the lessee (user) to pay the lessor (owner) for use of an asset.	Lease
Can an unlicensed assistant make a listing presentation?	No
Can a salesperson accept compensation from their sponsoring broker?	Yes
Can a flip tax be imposed on a cooperative property?	Yes
Business practice of U.S. real estate agents and building developers meant to encourage white property owners to sell their houses at a loss,	Blockbusting
Are blind ads legal?	No
An exchange of promises in which the terms by which the parties agree to be bound are declared either orally or in writing, or a combination of both, at the time it is made.	Express contract
An examination of the prices at which similar properties in the same area recently sold.	Comparative market analysis
An encumbrance is a right to, interest in, or legal liability on real property that does not prohibit passing title to the property but that diminishes its value. (T/F)	TRUE
An apartment information vendor is licensed by...	Department of Banking & Insurance
An agreement created by actions of the parties involved, but it is not written or spoken.	Implied contract
An agent who is authorized by the principal to perform any and all acts associated with the on-going operation of the job or business.	General agent

Agency created by written or oral agreement between the principal and the agent	Express agency
A written or spoken agreement, especially one concerning employment, sales, or tenancy, that is intended to be enforceable by law.	Contract
A type of zoning variance where a parcel of land may be given an exception from current zoning ordinances due to improvements made by a prior owner.	Nonconforming use
A reproduction of a technical drawing, documenting an architecture or an engineering design.	Blueprint
A real estate salesperson's compensation is set by...	Agreement between broker and salesperson.
A mortgage which covers two or more pieces of real estate.	Blanket Mortgage
A list of all the legal actions that have been performed or used in conjunction with a piece of property.	Abstract of title
A listing whereby an owner lists the property for sale with a number of brokers.	Open listing
A law passed by Congress in 1890. It prohibits certain business activities that federal government regulators deem to be anti-competitive.	The Sherman Antitrust Law
A home sold for $400,000. The Broker received $32,000. What rate of Commission did this broker charge?	8.00%
A debt instrument, secured by the collateral of specified real estate property, that the borrower is obliged to pay back with a predetermined set of payments.	Mortgage

A buyer should be cautious not to reveal the top asking price they are willing to pay to a ...	Seller's agent

Chapter 5

Practice Test 1

1. The document that gives a person the authorization to act on behalf of another is

A   disclosure with informed consent

B   power of attorney

C   attorney in fact

D   agency acknowledgment

2. Which of the following is not considered a fiduciary duty?

A   Loyalty

B   Confidentiality

C   Accountability

D   Assumability

3. A Subagent represents the

A   buyer

B   seller

C   government

D   none of the above

4. A Co-broke is where

A   an office lists and sells the same property

B   two offices are involved in the listing and selling of the same property

C   an office goes broke in the real estate business

D   company brokerage that does business

5. Which ownership contains the Right of Survivorship?

A   tenancy by Entirety

B   tenancy in Common

C   Joint Tenancy

D   both A and C

6. Which type of ownership has a condition of married at the time of purchase?

A   ownership in severalty

B   tenancy in common

C   joint tenancy

D   tenancy by entirety

7. Which is the best deed for the grantee?

A   Warranty Deed

B   Bargain and Sale Deed

C   Quitclaim Deed

D   Judicial Deed

8. The engineer that draws the dimensions of the land is called a(n)

A   engineer of drawing

B   surveyor

C   blue-printer

D   appraiser

9. An encumbrance is also known as

A   anything that lessens the bundle of rights to property

B   an inconvenience

C   a disturbance

D   a nuisance

10. A lien is

A   a violation

B   a claim or charge against something or someone

C   lawsuit against someone

D   a foreclosure action

11. Another term for transfer is

A   alliance

B   alienation

C   avoidance

D   attitude

12. A freehold estate is a

A   personal property interest

B   real property interest

C   temporary property interest

D   rental property interest

13. A leasehold estate is a

A   personal property interest

B   real property interest

C   forever property interest

D   rental property interest

14. The only time the grantee signs the deed is when

A   the grantee backs out of the sale

B   the grantee assumes the grantors mortgage

C   the grantee pays all cash for the property

D   the grantee purchases furniture along with the property

15. Actual eviction means

A   the tenant evicts themselves

B   the landlord illegally changes the locks

C   the landlord evicts the tenant through the legal process

D   an eviction goes wrong

16. What is the term when no specific end date is defined in a lease, but there is a repeated agreed-upon interval?

A   estate for years

B   periodic estate

C   estate at will

D   estate at sufferance

17. A freehold estate is

A   permanent ownership

B   temporary ownership

C   periodic ownership

D   sometime ownership

18. The Multiple Listing Service is a

A   government program

B   service for cooperating brokerages

C   service for elderly people

D   program for unemployed agents

19. What type of listing is it, when a seller must pay commission to an agent, no matter who sells the property?

A   an open listing

B   an exclusive agency listing

C   an exclusive right to sell

D   all of the above

20. Which listing is illegal to practice in Wyoming?

A   net listing

B   gross listing

C   sub listing

D   contract listing

21. An owner who seeks a mortgage loan that includes 3 properties is what type of mortgage?

A   a blanket mortgage

B   an FHA mortgage

C   a wraparound mortgage

D   a chattel mortgage

22. A junior mortgage is

A   a lien on personal property

B   the first mortgage recorded

C   always made by the seller

D   a lien after the first mortgage (usually a second mortgage)

23. Which of the following is an attachment that gives a lender the right to seize the personal property of a borrower who has not fulfilled their obligations of a loan?

A   general lien

B   mechanic's lien

C   specific lien

D   acceleration lien

24. The lien that is paid first in a court auction is which of the following?

A   real estate tax

B   mortgage

C   mechanic's

D   materialmen's

25. A deed is usually recorded at

A   the State Department

B   the Department of Banking & insurance

C   the county clerk courthouse

D   the lawyer's office

26. Real estate appraisers are licensed by the

A   Association of Appraisers

B   Banking Department

C   Commerce Dept.

D   State

27. Which of the following is seller financing?

A   sales financing

B   personal loan

C   primary mortgage

D   purchase money mortgage

28. How old must one be to qualify for a reverse annuity mortgage?

A   65

B   62

C   60

D   55

29. What approach does an appraiser use to estimate the value of a 1 - 4 unit dwelling?

A   cost

B   income

C   sales comparison

D   investment

30. The number of square feet in 1 square yard is

A   3

B   4

C   9

D   5

31. An appraisal report must be

A   verbal with witnesses

B   in writing

C   on legal paper

D   sent to the seller and buyer

32. A mortgage is a

A   involuntary lien

B   voluntary lien

C   custom lien

D   purpose lien

33. Assessed value is usually used by the

A   bank

B   lender

C   government

D   appraiser

34. The process of combining adjacent parcels of land to form one larger parcel is

A   parcel

B   assemblage

C   sub-division

D   plot

35. The engineer that draws an aerial view of the lot is known as the

A   civil engineer

B   mechanical engineer

C   land surveyor

D   land engineer

36. Which appraisal approach can be used for an apartment building?

A   Direct sales comparison

B   Cost approach

C   Income approach

D   Insured approach

37. The land owner that has the right to use an easement over another person's land is

A   servient

B   dominant

C   ownership rights

D   encroachment

38. A visual easement is called

A   affirmative

B   negative

C   subtract

D   relay

39. Regulation Z does not cover which of the following properties?

A   1 unit family dwelling

B   2 unit family dwelling

C   commercial

D   residential

40. Something of value in a contract is called

A   credit

B   consideration

C   deposit

D   prorations

41. The starting point in drawing a survey is called

A   metes & bounds

B   starting point

C   point of origin

D   point start

42. A licensee can lose their license for

A   representing a client

B   qualifying a buyer before showing a property

C   doing a credit check on a potential tenant

D   commingling funds of clients

43. Which of the following is NOT realty?

A   Fee simple estate

B   Freehold estate

C   Timber

D   Life Estate

44. What is the term that describes government taking private property for public use?

A   encroachment

B   easement

C   eminent domain

D   novation

45. The landlord of a lease is called the

A   grantor

B   grantee

C   lessor

D   lessee

46. Rent for a 50 by 80 feet office is $830 per month. What is the annual rent per square foot?

A $2.49

B $10.37

C $4.00

D $16.60

47. Which of the following is an example of the bundle of rights?

A   mortgage

B   air rights

C   leases

D   all of the above

48. Which method of advertising is usually the most expensive?

A   newspapers

B   magazines

C   radio and TV

D   word of mouth

49. A lot is 2.5 acres. How many square feet is that?

A   66,750

B   103,900

C   111,400

D   108,900

50. Which fiduciary duty is involved when temporarily holding someone's money?

A   disclosure

B   loyalty

C   accountability

D   confidentiality

51. Another type of exclusive listing other than an exclusive agency listing is called an

A   Exclusive Right to Sell

B   Exclusive Selling Listing

C   Exclusive Tenancy

D   Exclusive Open Listing

52. The Statute(s) agents follow when conducting real estate services is:

A   Title 98A, Chapter 23

B   Article 78A

C   Title 33, Chapter 28

D   Article 62A

53. A kickback is

A   allowable under certain instances

B   only allowable if the seller agrees

C   illegal to take

D   none of the above

54. A severe crime is called a

A   Violation

B   Lien

C   Felony

D   Misdemeanor

55. A client should receive

A   Full Representation & Service

B   Only Acknowledgment

C   Full Attention

D   Client Privileges

56. A trustee represents the

A   beneficiary

B   seller

C   buyer

D   sales agent

57. Which is the statute that governs real estate Licensees in WY?

A   Article 9A

B   Article 7B

C   Title 33: Chapter 28

D   Article 12A

58. Real estate professionals are required to take how many hours of continuing education every cycle?

A   20

B   45

C   17.5

D   12

59. What is the term when another state will recognize the qualifications and education held by a Wyoming licensee when applying for a real estate license in that state?

A   exchange

B   reciprocal

C   novation

D   escheat

60. What is the license which allows one to deal with apartments and charge fees?

A   apartment showing vendor

B   apartment rental person

C   apartment exchange agent

D   apartment information vendor

61. Who can sell real estate and charge a fee without a license?

A   auctioneer

B   property manager

C   for sale by owner

D   attorney

62. For a deed to be recorded, it must be in writing and:

A   signed by the grantee

B   delivered immediately to the court

C   signed by the grantor(s)

D   have at least 2 grantors

63. Which of the following is a choice for a broker license?

A   single

B   substitute

C   implied

D   associate

64. Which of the following is the term for allowing a change to occur in a real estate transaction between two or more parties?

A   disclosure with informed consent

B   allowment in writing

C   statute of frauds

D   consent by agency

65. A broker can charge commission from both the seller and buyer only if

A   the buyer is a friend

B   the seller gets an offer above the listing price

C   all parties are aware of the situation

D   it is paid in cash

66. Another term for the transfer of real property is:

A   alienation

B   condemnation

C   escheat

D   implied

67. A deed must

A   show the legal usage of the structure

B   show the selling price of the house

C   be in writing

D   be recorded

68. Real estate plus the _____ results in real property.

A   land

B   fixtures

C   trees

D   bundle of rights

69. Another term for personal property is

A   mobile

B   trade

C   chattel

D   alienation

70. Which of the following terms defines when one entity controls a certain market?

A   status

B   constitute

C   gross profit

D   monopoly

71. A percentage lease usually occurs

A   in a parking lot

B   in an apartment building

C   in a shopping mall

D   in a home rental

72. All of the following are government agents in the secondary mortgage market EXCEPT

A   FNMA.

B   HUD.

C   FHLMC.

D   GNMA.

73. A pro forma is a

A   Report of a property's actual past income - generating performance.

B   Measurement of the degree of investor involvement.

C   Projection of a property's likely performance in the future.

D   Device for calculating the effect of leveraging on accelerated depreciation.

74. An estate at will is

A   A limited partnership

B   A tenancy of uncertain duration

C   An inheritance by will

D   A life tenancy

75. All of the following are fiduciary duties owed by an agent to a principal EXCEPT

A   Loyalty.

B   Accounting.

C   Obedience.

D   Interest.

Chapter 6

Answers: Practice Test 1

1. B.

A power of attorney gives you the authority to act on behalf of another.

2. D.

The fiduciary duties an agent owes to a client are care, obedience, loyalty, disclosure, accountability and confidentiality.

3. B.

A subagent represents the broker's client.

4. B.

Both brokerages cooperate in the sale of the property.

5. D.

Tenancy in common does not include the right of survivorship, therefore ownership can be inherited.

6. D.

The purchasers must be married to co-own as tenants by the entirety.

7. A.

The general warranty deed provides the grantee with the most guarantees.

8. B.

A survey will identify the boundaries and area of a parcel of land.

9. A.

An encumbrance is an imperfection on title to land.

10. B.

A lien is a charge against a property that provides security for a debt.

11. B.

Alienation is transferring property to another.

12. B.

A freehold estate is ownership for an indeterminate length of time.

13. A.

A leasehold estate is a tenant's right to occupy real estate.

14. B.

The grantee will assume all liabilities of the existing mortgage.

15. C.

Actual eviction is the legal process for removing a tenant from the premises.

16. B.

A periodic estate would be a week to week, month to month or year to year tenancy.

17. A.

A freehold estate is ownership in land for an indeterminate length of time.

18. B.

The MLS is a data base of listings in a specific area for brokerages to cooperate in the sale of the listings

19. C.

The listing brokerage will earn commission no matter who brings the buyer. The brokerage will earn commission even if the seller finds the buyer.

20. A.

The broker will earn any amount of money over a set sales price as commission. This will pit the broker's commission against the seller's net proceeds.

21. A.

A blanket mortgage will encumber more than one property. Subdividers commonly use this type of mortgage

22. D.

A junior mortgage is one that is subordinate to an existing lien on the same property. Priority is usually set by recording date.

23. A.

A general lien attaches to the person and all that they own.

24. A.

Real estate taxes take priority over other liens.

25. C.

Properties are recorded in the county which they are physically located.

26. D.

Appraisers have to be licensed for many federally related transactions and also are required to be licensed or certified by the state.

27. D.

A purchase money mortgage is seller financing.

28. B.

To qualify for a reverse annuity mortgage the person must be 62 or older.

29 C.

Up to a four unit dwelling is residential.

30. C.

3 feet x 3 feet = 9 square feet

31. B.

The appraisal report should be in writing to be used as an estimate of value with a loan.

32. B.

The borrower would voluntarily give the lien to the lender as security for the loan.

33. C.

Assessed value is usually used when calculating property tax.

34. B.

Combined parcels for a greater value is plottage. The process is assemblage.

35. C.

The surveyor will outline the property boundaries.

36. C.

An apartment building is an income producing building

37. B.

The dominant estate benefits from the easement.

38. B.

A visual easement is referred to as being 'negative'.

39. C.

Regulation Z regulates residential transactions.

40. B.

Consideration maybe money, love and affection, nominal or something of value.

41. C.

Sometimes called the point of beginning.

42. D.

Commingling is mixing client funds with personal or brokerage operation funds.

43. C.

Timber is severed from the land, making it personal property.

44. C.

Eminent Domain is the government's right to take private property for a public use.

45. C.

The lessor is the owner.

46. A.

$830 x 12 = $9960 rent/year 50' x 80' = 4000 square feet $9960/4000 sq ft = $2.49 per sq ft

47. D.

The bundle of rights consists of possession, enjoyment, disposition, control and exclusion

48. C.

Radio and television are most costly.

49. D.

2.5 * 43560 sq ft. = 108,900 square feet.

50. C.

An agent must be able to account for all monies received from a client.

51. A.

The exclusive right to sell listing provides maximum protection for the brokerage.

52. C.

Title 33, Chapter 28 is the Wyoming State Real Property Law

53. C.

A kickback is an unearned fee for services not provided.

54. C.

A felony is a serious violation. More severe than a misdemeanor.

55. A.

An agent should provide all fiduciary duties to a client.

56. A.

The beneficiary is the lender.

Actual eviction is a legal process that removes the tenant from the premises.

57. C.

Title 33: Chapter 28 is the statute that governs real estate licensee in WY.

58. B.

Real Estate Professionals are required to take 45 hours of continuing education every three years.

59. B.

The law of reciprocity allows you to use your real estate license education and qualifications in other states while applying for a license in that state.

60. D.

These individuals pay a fee for licensing and they are only able to post information about available apartments.

61. D.

An Attorney has the right to act as a real estate broker by holding a law license. If an attorney chooses to hire agents, they must apply for a broker's license.

62. C.

For a deed to be considered valid the Grantor (owner) must sign the deed. The Grantee does not have to sign the deed for it to be a valid transfer

63. D.

An associate broker is one that has the credentials to be a licensed broker but chooses to work under another broker

64. A.

Changes can be made to any real estate transaction as long as all parties are informed and all parties agree to the change. We call this disclosure with informed consent

65. C.

A broker can charge both sides of the transaction as long as all parties to the transaction are aware and give consent.

66. A.

Alienation is the giving or transfer of real property to another.

67. C.

All deeds must be in writing to be valid. A deed does not have to be recorded to be valid.

68. D.

Real property is more than just the land itself, it also includes the RIGHTS that come with ownership. These rights are possession, control, enjoyment, exclude and disposition.

69. C.

Personal property is all that does not fit the definition of real property. Sometimes also called chattel.

70. D.

A monopoly is when one company controls the entire market.

71. C.

A percentage lease is when a retailer pays a land owner a percentage of the earnings. This is most common in retail because the landlord is partially responsible for bringing the traffic to the store location.

72. B.

The Department of Housing and Urban Development (HUD) is a U.S. government agency created in 1965 to support community development and home ownership.

73. C.

A proforma is a projection of a property's future performance.

74. B.

 An estate at will is a leasehold estate where the tenant possesses the property for an indefinite amount of time. The lease can be terminated by either party at any time.

75. D.

Interest is not one of the responsibilities.

Chapter 7

Practice Test 2

1. Real Estate License Laws were instituted to

A   raise revenue through license fees

B   protect the public and maintain high standards

C   limit the number of Brokers and Salespersons

D   match the federal government's requirement

2. In Wyoming, real estate licenses are under the supervision of the

A   Department of Education

B   Real Estate Commission

C   Board of REALTORS

D   Department of State

3. A fully qualified broker who chooses to act as a salesperson under another broker's sponsorship is licensed as a(n):

A   adjunct salesperson

B   associate broker

C   principal broker

D   sales associate

4. A broker must have completed how many hours of prescribed study for licensing?

A   22.5

B   30

C   45

D   120

5. Salesperson James told the telephone company to print the following ad under Real Estate in the Yellow Pages: Beth Smith, Licensed Salesperson, Residential Property, 718-555-4973. He should have included his

A   age

B   cell number

C   license number

D   brokerage name

6. A violation of license law is legally classified as a(n):

A   infraction

B   offense

C   misdemeanor

D   felony

7. If a principal broker loses their license, the associated salespeople must immediately

A   move the office to another location

B   appoint one of their members to supervise

C   obtain a broker's license

D   stop listing and selling

8. How many years must a real estate broker keep all documents pertaining to a real estate transaction?

A   three years

B   five years

C   two years

D   indefinitely

9. The term commingling pertains to

A   soliciting the services of another broker's salesperson

B   failing to deliver copies of contracts to a client

C   mixing the broker's funds with escrow deposits

D   promoting business at social gatherings

10. A buyer's broker is told by the buyer that he had filed for bankruptcy the year before. The buyer's broker

A   can politely refuse to provide any information to the seller that would violate her duty of confidentiality to the buyer

B   should discuss with the buyer her duty to reveal the bankruptcy to the MLS

C   has a duty of fair dealing toward the seller and must discuss the buyer's finances

D   has no responsibility to the seller, because she is the buyer's agent

11. Broker Joe owes customer Kelly Moore

A   loyalty

B   fairness and honesty

C   confidentiality

D   accounting

12. The Agency Disclosure form must be presented, explained and signed when

A   the customer makes an offer

B   the seller accepts an offer

C   the seller and buyer first meet

D   there is a first substantial contact

13. Brokers have the most incentive to market a property when they have a(n):

A   open listing

B   exclusive-agency listing

C   exclusive right-to-sell listing

D   net listing

14. A specific tract of land is known as a

A   devise

B   chattel

C   parcel

D   littoral

15. Tim Rooney, owner of a farm in Putnam County, has found that an oil company wants to lease his

A   littoral rights

B   prior appropriation rights

C   riparian rights

D   subsurface rights

16. When a bridge is to be constructed over and above the land, the contractor purchases the landowner's

A   riparian rights

B   subsurface rights

C   air rights

D   littoral rights

17. Millie Kim owns land along the River, as the owner she has certain water rights called

A   subsurface rights

B   riparian rights

C   air rights

D   littoral rights

18. Jim's mechanic's lien will remain against the property for at least:

A   one year

B   eight months

C   ten year

D   four months

19. A telephone company has a right to install its poles and wires granted by what type of easement?

A   by necessity

B   in gross

C   by prescription

D   appurtenant

20. When someone dies leaving no will and no natural heirs, the Wyoming State property goes to

A   the federal government

B   local charities

C   the state of Wyoming

D   an escrow fund

21. To place a lien against personal property, one must file a

A   UCC filing

B   security bond

C   mortgage lien

D   insurance policy

22. Which of the following is not a legal description?

A   the street address

B   the rectangular survey

C   block and lot

D   metes and bounds

23. It is essential that every deed be signed by the

A   devisee

B   grantee

C   grantor and grantee

D   grantor

24. Consideration in a deed refers to

A   gentle handling of the document

B   the habendum clause

C   something of value given

D   estoppel

25. A notary's acknowledgment of the signature on a deed is necessary

A   for the deed to be recorded

B   before a transfer tax can be paid

C   to prove that the seller wishes to sell

D   for the deed to be valid

26. If a licensee has wrongfully obtained funds in the course of a violation of license law, DOS may impose a fine of

A   up to three times the amount received

B   up to four times the amount received

C   the full amount received

D $1000 or the full amount received

27. Which of the following is NOT exempt from completing continuing education requirements?

A   broker for 15 years before July 2008

B   attorney licensed to practice in Wyoming

C   broker for 20 years before 7/2008

D   salesperson licensed for 15 years

28. A broker who conducts business as a sole proprietorship under an assumed name is classified as a(n):

A   associate broker

B   trade name broker

C   individual broker

D   corporate broker

29. A partner in a real estate firm must hold which level of license?

A   associate broker

B   salesperson

C   broker

D   broker plus two years of experience

30. A business activity involving a monopoly or conspiracy that negatively impacts another individual or company is called a(n):

A   estoppel

B   illegal use of the rule of reason

C   restraint of trade

D   kickback

31. In Wyoming, dual agency is

A   a violation of the license law

B   allowable under Wyoming law with disclosure and informed consent

C   allowable with respect to commercial transactions only

D   a violation of the agency laws of Wyoming

32. An attorney-in-fact

A   must be an attorney at law

B   is appointed by court order

C   is appointed by a power of attorney

D   is appointed to supervise a foreclosure sale

33. The relationship between a broker and a salesperson is commonly

A   vendor and vendee

B   principal and agent

C   grantor and grantee

D   management and labor agent

34. The principal amount of an assumed mortgage appears on the buyer's statement as a

A   debit

B   reconciliation

C   credit

D   format

35. A blanket mortgage usually encumbers

A   an underlying wraparound mortgage

B   several mortgages

C   several parcels of real property

D   household goods

36. A freehold estate limited by the holder's own lifetime is a

A   life estate pur autre vie

B   life estate

C   life estate in remainder

D   life estate in reversion

37. A cooperative apartment is characterized by

A   fee simple ownership

B   ownership of stock in a corporation

C   joint tenancy ownership of the land

D   individual freehold estate

38. The legal right to enter upon another's property is a(n)

A   trespass

B   encroachments

C   easement

D   variance

39. Which of the following is NOT a characteristic of a license?

A   personal privilege

B   interest in the land

C   revocable privilege

D   non-assignable

40. The giving of real property from the state or government to a private individual is known as

A   dedication

B   eminent domain

C   public grant

D   escheat

41. A deed in which the wording in the granting clause contains "remise and release" is which of the following?

A   special warranty

B   quickclaim deed

C   grant, bargain and sale deed

D   quitclaim deed

42. The person appointed by a court to distribute the property of a person dying intestate is a(n):

A   probate

B   executor

C   administrator

D   devisee

43. What should the property manager and owner sign to manage the property?

A   management analysis

B   management statement

C   management agreement

D   management proposal

44. A lease that provides for the lessee to pay a part or all of the expenses of a property, in addition to rent, is called a(n):

A   estate at sufferance

B   sale and leaseback

C   net lease

D   gross lease

45. Another name for actual eviction is

A   legal process

B   constructive eviction

C   reversion

D   litigation of damages

46. When a purchaser and seller have a valid contract for the sale of real property, the purchaser has

A   legal title

B   no title

C   constructive title

D   equitable title

47. Wyoming State law requires agency to be disclosed by

A   the first substantive contact

B   a, c & d

C   the acceptance of a purchase contract

D   a time prior to the signing of a listing

48. The persons often involved in an agency are

A   principal

B   agent

C   a & b

D   third party

49. Michael Jones was not paid for roofing the Lyon's home. How long does he have to file a mechanic's lien?

A   eight months

B   one year

C   four months

D   two years

50. Kim buys a summer cottage that has a mechanic's lien against it. The lien was placed by the workman who was not paid by the former owner David, for constructing a dock. The lien

A   is void

B   is Jim's responsibility only

C   remains as a claim against the property

D   is considered satisfied

51. A home was purchased in 2005 for $425,000. It was sold recently for $478,000. What is the rate of return on the profit for this house?

A   12.47%

B   1.12 %

C   88.91%

D   53%

52. To establish an easement by prescription in Wyoming, a person must use another's property for an uninterrupted period of

A   five years

B   fifteen years

C   Twenty years

D   ten years

53. Jim's neighbor, Ed, regularly uses Jim's driveway to reach his garage. Ed has an easement over Jim's driveway. Jim's property is called

A   the dominant estate

B   an estate

C   a leasehold

D   the servient estate

54. A shared driveway agreement will probably take the form of a(n)

A   voluntary lien

B   affidavit of entitlement

C   easement appurtenant

D   certificate of usage

55. A party wall

A   is located only on a servient estate

B   faces a main road

C   straddles a boundary line

D   is owned by one party

56. The lien with first claim against real estate is

A   a mechanic's lien

B   whatever lien was first recorded

C   a first mortgage

D   the property tax

57. A house is sold for $190,000. It is then appraised for $185,000. If the bank is willing to lend an 80% LTV, how much of a down payment will the buyer be required to make?

A $ 42,000

B $ 37,000

C $ 38,000

D $ 40,000

58. If Sam Flanner buys a new home in the Lawrence County subdivision known as Sound Ridge, his land probably bears a legal description based on

A   the recorded plat

B   metes and bounds

C   the rectangular survey

D   the street address

59. What is the interest rate on a $10,000 loan with a $125 monthly interest?

A   2.5%

B   15%

C   7.5%

D   10%

60. A house sells for $195,000. The total commission rate is 6%, of which the listing office receives 2.5% and the selling office 3.5%.

Susan, the selling agent, receives a 60% split of the selling office commission. How much will she earn as commission?

A $ 2,437.50

B $ 11,700.00

C $ 9,750.00

D $ 4,095.00

61. A lot is 425 feet by 425 feet. How many acres is that?

A   2.4 acres

B   1.6 acres

C   4.1 acres

D   8.4 acres

62. A declaration before a notary public, providing evidence that a signature is genuine, is which of the following?

A   affidavit

B   acknowledgment

C   affirmation

D   estoppel

63. A lease is considered to be

A   a freehold estate

B   fee simple

C   real property

D   personal property

64. A tenant's lease has expired. The tenant has not left or negotiated a renewal lease. The landlord does not want the tenant to remain. These circumstances have created which type of tenancy?

A   periodic estate

B   tenancy at will

C   estate for years

D   tenancy at sufferance

65. Jasper Jones fears that if the building is sold, a new landlord may not honor the year remaining on his apartment lease. The new owner

A   must abide by the terms of her original lease

B   would have to give her 90 days notice to move

C   must honor the lease but may charge double rent

D   can terminate her rental only if he intends to occupy the apartment himself

66. Bob Lyon's apartment lease agreement states that it will expire on April 30, 2009. When must the landlord give notice that him tenancy is about to terminate?

A   January 31, 2006

B   No notice is required

C   February 31, 2006

D   April 1, 2009

67. What will the tenant pay with a triple net lease?

A   everything but the mortgage

B   rent only

C   rent plus a share of the business profits

D   rent plus any increase in property taxes

68. A ground lease is usually

A   terminated with 30 days notice

B   long term

C   based on percentages

D   a net lease

69. The landlord must furnish a lead paint information booklet

A   within 100 days after the lease is signed

B   for residential buildings constructed before 1978

C   if the building is intended exclusively for those over 55

D   only if the building contains six or more units

70. Jim manufactures kites in a small rented building. In addition to monthly rent, he pays heat, electric, and property taxes on the building. She probably has a

A   periodic lease

B   net lease

C   percentage lease

D   security lease

71. Mark Burns drives into a gas station and fills up his gas tank. He is obligated to pay for the fuel through which type of contract?

A   express

B   implied

C   oral

D   voidable

72. A contract is said to be bilateral when

A   there are two sellers and two buyers

B   one of the parties is a minor

C   all parties to the contract are bound to act

D   only one party to the agreement is bound to act

73. Which of the following would have to be licensed as a real estate broker or salesperson to act in a real estate transaction on behalf of another for a fee?

A   attorney licensed in Wyoming

B   executor of an estate

C   an auctioneer

D   referee acting under court order

74. Freehold estates include all of the following EXCEPT a

A   Fee Simple Estate.

B   Qualified Fee Estate.

C   Leasehold Estate.

D   Life Estate.

75. An agent who mixes clients funds with their own personal funds is engaging in

A   Estoppel.

B   Escrow.

C   Commingling.

D   Misrepresentation.

Chapter 8

Answers: Practice Test 2

1. B.

The licensing laws are created to protect the public from unethical practices in real estate.

2. B.

The Wyoming Real Estate Commission.

3. B.

The associate broker is not the broker of record for the company.

4. D.

A broker needs to have 150 hours of prescribed study

5. D.

The brokerage name must be included in all advertising.

6. C.

A violation of licensing law is a misdemeanor.

7. D.

Business is done under the brokerage name. If a principal broker loses their license, all real estate activity must stop.

8. A.

All real estate transaction records must be kept for three years.

9. C.

Commingling is mixing client funds with office operation funds or personal funds. Client monies must remain separate.

10. A.

The buyer's agent must remain loyal to the buyer and cannot share confidential information about their client.

11. B.

An agent still owes a customer fair and honest dealing.

12. D.

Commonly many state laws require disclosure of agency before any confidential information is disclosed about a person's motivation or finances.

13. C.

The exclusive right to sell listing provides the brokerage with maximum protection. The listing brokerage will earn commission no matter who sells the property.

14. C.

A parcel is an identifiable tract of land.

15. D.

Subsurface rights include mineral, water, gas and oil beneath the surface of the land.

16. C.

Air rights can be purchased or leased by another.

17. B.

Riparian rights are water rights along a flowing body of water.

18. A.

A mechanic's lien is for material suppliers or laborers and contractors that have not been paid for their materials or labor.

19. B.

An easement in gross is an individual or company interest or right to use the land of another. Commonly a utility easement.

20. C.

This is called escheat. A person dies intestate and has no living heirs, the property reverts to the state.

21. A.

The Uniform Commercial code filing is a legal form that creditors file that it has an interest in a debtor's personal property. A lien on the personal property.

22. A.

A street address does not define the perimeter and boundaries of a parcel of real estate.

23. D.

The grantor must sign a deed. The grantee does not have to sign a deed.

24. C.

Consideration is something of value. Money, love and affection and nominal are examples.

25. A.

The notary will make sure the grantor's signature is genuine and of their own free will.

26. D.

The amount will be at the discretion of the state.

27. D.

The others are exempt.

28. B.

The broker would have to disclose to the state doing business as, then provide the name.

29. C.

To be a partner, the person must hold a broker's license.

30. C.

These activities would violate the antitrust laws. These laws are designed to preserve the free enterprise of the open market.

31. B.

Dual agency must have the consent of both parties to the transaction.

32. C.

The power of attorney is a document authorizing an individual to act as an agent for another.

33. B.

The salesperson is an agent of the broker. The broker is the agent of the buyer or seller.

34. C.

The buyer will assume the debt and obligations that come with it.

35. C.

A blanket mortgage covers more than one parcel of land.

36. B.

A life estate is an interest in real estate that is limited to the lifetime of its owner. A reversion or remainder interest is a future interest in the real property.

37. B.

In a cooperative apartment, the occupants will own stock in the corporation and in return receive a proprietary lease to the unit.

38. C.

An easement right is a legal right to use the land of another for a specific purpose.

39. B.

A license is a privilege to use another's property and may be revoked.

40. C.

A transfer from the government to a private individual is accomplished by a public grant.

41. D.

A quitclaim deed carries no warranties.

42. C.

An executor is named in a will. The administrator is appointed by the court.

43. C.

A property management agreement should be signed prior to the property manager managing the property for the owner. The agreement will define the obligations of both parties.

44. C.

A few of the expenses the tenant would be expected to pay are taxes, insurance, utilities and repairs.

45. A.

Eviction is a legal process to remove a tenant from the premises.

46. D.

Equitable title is acquired by the buyer after the sales contract is executed. Legal title has not transferred.

47. B.

Agency disclosure laws are dictated by state law. The agent must disclose the parties they represent.

48. C.

The third party is the customer.

49. C.

A mechanic's lien is for contractors, laborers and material suppliers who have performed work or supplied materials and was not paid for the labor or materials.

50. C.

The lien attaches to the property and will remain attached through a transfer.

51. A.

$478,000 - $425,000 = $53,000/$425,000 = 12.47%

52. D.

The prescribed period of time is ten years.

53. D.

The servient estate is the estate that is burdened by the easement

54. C.

An easement appurtenant will run with the land and go to future owners of the property.

55. C.

A party wall is a shared wall between two adjacent parcels of land.

56. D.

Property taxes and special assessments take priority over other liens and will be paid first.

57. B.

The lender will base the value on the lower value between appraised value and sales price. 185,000 x 20% = $37,000

58. A.

A street address is not a legal description.

59. B.

$125 x 12 = $1500 interest per year $1500/$10,000 = 15%

60. D.

$195,000 x 3.5% = $6825 x 60% = $4095

61. C.

425 feet * 425 feet = 180625 square feet. 180625 sq ft / 43560 sq ft = 4.1 acres.

$600,000 x 1.425% = $8550 $600,000/500 = 1200 x $2 = $2400 $8550 + $2400 = $10,950

62.B.

The purpose of an acknowledgment is to make sure the signature is genuine and of their own free will.

63. D.

The tenant does not have ownership in a lease. They only have the right to occupy the premises.

64. D.

An estate at sufferance is when a tenant continues to occupy the premises after the lease rights have expired.

65. A.

The sale will not terminate the lease.

66. B.

The lease has a definite termination date. The type of lease is an estate for years and no notice is required

67. A.

The tenant will pay maintenance fees, taxes, insurance, utilities and repairs.

68. B.

A ground lease is a long term lease of land on which the tenant usually owns the building.

69.B.

Any residential construction prior to 1978 must provide the buyer or tenant with a lead paint disclosure pamphlet.

70. B.

The tenant will pay some or all of the expenses with a net lease.

71. B.

An implied contract is created by a person's actions.

72. C.

A bilateral contract contains two binding promises.

73. C.

An auctioneer would have to be licensed as a real estate broker or salesperson.

74. C.

A leasehold estate is a personal property interest.

75. C.

The individual is engaging in commingling which is illegal.

Chapter 9

Practice Test 3

1. Freehold estates include all of the following EXCEPT a

A   Fee Simple Estate.

B   Qualified Fee Estate.

C   Leasehold Estate.

D   Life Estate.

2. Joy, David, and Michael own a property as tenants in common. David sells his share of ownership to John. John is now a(n):

A   Joint tenant with Joy and Michael.

B   Tenant in common with Joy and Michael.

C   Owner in severalty.

D   Qualified fee owner.

3. The action taken by the state to take property when a property owner dies without heirs and without a will is called?

A   Eminent Domain.

B   Escheat.

C   Foreclosure.

D   Adverse Possession.

4. The tax due on profits realized on the sale of investment property, held by the owner for six years and six months, is called

A   Short-term capital gains.

B   Long-term capital gains.

C   Profit margin tax.

D   Property appreciation tax.

5. The type of insurance that protects a landlord from liability damages due to criminal or negligent acts of an employee during working hours is

A   Homeowner's insurance.

B   A surety bond.

C   FEMA insurance

D   All-purpose insurance.

6. A naturally occurring gas that can present itself as an environmental hazard is

A   PCBs.

B   Carbon Monoxide.

C   Radon.

D   Friable Asbestos.

7. The Comprehensive Environmental Response, Compensation, and Liability Act (CERCLA) provides

A   Pure drinking water.

B   Landowner liability for cleanup of environmental contamination.

C   Government funding to subsidize contaminant cleanup costs.

D   Radon emissions controls.

8. A tenant who qualifies for Section 8 housing and earns $12,000 per year will have to pay a maximum monthly rent of

A   300

B   400

C   500

D   600

9. The city agency responsible for determination of land use is the

A   Department of Buildings.

B   Department of Finance.

C   City Planning Commission.

D   Landmarks Preservation Commission.

10. In Trenton, the agency responsible for enacting local laws is

A   The Board of Trustees.

B   The City Planning Commission.

C   OPRHP.

D   The City Council.

11. When a newly constructed building is complete and passes inspection from a building department inspector, the city will issue a

A   Certificate of occupancy.

B   Certificate of completion.

C   Certificate of compliance.

D   Certificate of certiorari.

12. An ad valorem tax is based on

A   Value of city improvements to a neighborhood.

B   Assessed property value.

C   Average home values in a neighborhood.

D   Use of an equalization factor.

13. Real estate taxes are based on

A   Tax shares owned by the property owner.

B   Homestead rates.

C   Budget requirements.

D   Certiorari rates.

14. A first-time home buyer may not be liable for a 10 percent early withdrawal penalty if he or she uses IRA funds to buy a home. This exemption allows the buyer to use IRA funds up to

A   5,000

B   10,000

C   15,000

D   20,000

15. The income a real estate salesperson earns from commissions paid on closed transactions is considered to be

A   Passive income.

B   Portfolio income.

C   Capital gains income.

D   Active income.

16. Which statement is always TRUE?

A   All encumbrances are liens.

B   All liens are encumbrances.

C   All liens are encroachments.

D   All easements are liens.

17. In Wyoming, the transfer tax on real property sales above 1 million equals

A $0.55 per $500 of the sales price.

B $2.00 per $500 of the sales price.

C $2.55 per $500 of the sales price.

D   None.

18. An abstract of title is a document that

A   Is used to transfer the title to real property.

B   Offers a summary of the history of the recorded title.

C   Guarantees that the grantor has marketable title.

D   Insures the title against third-party claims.

19. A closing takes place on October 18. The annual property taxes are $4,500 and are paid at the end of each year. On the closing statement, the buyer will be credited and the seller will be debited

A $900.

B $3,587.50.

C $3,812.

D $1,125.

20. Colleges, hospitals, and houses of worship are examples of

A   Commercial real estate.

B   Special-purpose property.

C   Residential property.

D   Mixed-use property.

21. Neighbors are allowed to express their concerns in public hearings when a developer applies for a

A   Variance.

B   Conditional-use permit.

C   Nonconforming-use permit.

D   Tax exemption.

22. Regulations that govern permissible use of property are called

A   Building codes.

B   Environmental codes.

C   Planning codes.

D   Zoning codes.

23. A property owner wants to construct a building on designated wetlands. Before construction can start, permits and approvals must be obtained from

A   State of Wyoming.

B   The Environmental Protection Agency.

C   The Army Corps of Engineers.

D   All the above.

24. An appraisal of real property offers

A   An opinion of value.

B   The market value of a property.

C   The assessed value of property.

D   The sales price of the property.

25. A real estate broker who is not a licensed appraiser can offer an opinion of property value. That is called a

A   Sales value estimate.

B   Market comparison value.

C   Comparative market analysis.

D   Replacement value estimate.

26. A licensed appraiser uses three approaches to value in appraising a property, but each approach yields a different value for the same parcel. To determine the final appraised value, the final step in the appraisal process is

A   Omitting the highest value and averaging the two remaining values

B   Omitting the lowest value and averaging the two remaining values.

C   Reconciliation of the values by giving the most weight to the most appropriate approach to value.

D   Taking an average of all three values.

27. When appraising a school building for insurance purposes, the best approach in obtaining an appraised value of the property is the

A   Cost approach.

B   Income approach.

C   Market comparison approach.

D   Comparative market analysis approach.

28. The Cheyenne Executive Law covers discrimination against race, creed, color, national origin, sexual orientation, and

A   Marital Status.

B   Religion.

C   Steering.

D   Middle-Class families with children.

29. A home owner takes out a new fire insurance policy on their home. Fire insurance is a type of

A   Static risk.

B   Dynamic risk.

C   Limited liability risk.

D   Comprehensive risk.

30. A commercial building is fireproof, has a sprinkler system, a closed circuit security surveillance system, and a security fence around the building. The building would be categorized as a(n)

A   Dynamic risk.

B   Static risk.

C   HPR property.

D   Multi-peril risk.

31. A homeowner's insurance policy may not be issued if the

A   House has no alarm system.

B   Property is in an area with a high incidence of burglaries.

C   Property is outside a flood zone.

D   House is not owner-occupied.

32. The value of a property used to determine property taxes is the

A   Assessed value.

B   Replacement value.

C   Market value.

D   Appraised value.

33. The buyer of a foreclosed property at auction will become the owner of the property

A   Subject to satisfaction of all other liens.

B   After giving the occupant sufficient time to vacate.

C   With guarantee of habitability.

D   As soon as the new deed is delivered to and accepted by the buyer.

34. Cheyenne is allowed to divide property into four classes. A 50-unit condominium building would be included in

A   Class I

B   Class II

C   Class III

D   Class IV

35. Improvement value is determined by all of the following EXCEPT:

A   Age of the improvement.

B   Condition of the improvement.

C   Cost of the improvement.

D   Construction of the improvement.

36. A condominium building may be operated by a(n)

A   Board of managers.

B   Board of directors.

C   Advisory board.

D   Board of supervisors.

37. If a condominium owner wants to sell their unit, the condominium owner's association may have the right to

A   An option to buy the unit.

B   Veto the sale.

C   First refusal to buy the unit.

D   Determine the minimum acceptable sales price.

38. Before a building may be converted into a condominium, what documents must be filed with the county clerk's office?

A   An offering plan and a plat map.

B   A declaration and floor plans.

C   An offering statement and a red herring.

D   An application for zoning variance and blueprints of the building.

39. Rules that govern condominium home owners associations are called

A   Covenants.

B   Restrictions.

C   Easements

D   Bylaws.

40. An estimation of how much income an investment property will generate in the future appears on a(n)

A   Depreciation schedule.

B   Operating schedule.

C   Prediction schedule.

D   Pro forma schedule.

41. Debt service refers to

A   Operating expenses.

B   Real estate and income taxes.

C Principal and interest included in a mortgage payment.

D Vacancies and credit losses.

42. A recommended type of real estate investment for people who have little or no investment experience would be

A A vacant land.

B A one, two, or three-family house.

C A 20-unit condominium building.

D Fixer-upper properties.

43. Rate of return is directly related to

A Risk.

B Amount of money invested.

C The time it takes for an investment to break even.

D Terms of financing.

44. When calculating NOI, what item is NOT included?

A Management fees.

B Real estate taxes.

C Utility bills.

D Mortgage payments.

45. The Uniform Commercial Code (UCC) is

A Required for commercial property investors.

B   Commercial law adopted by every state.

C   Commercial law for international trade.

D   Federal regulations for commercial property developers.

46. A type of investment property that produces little or no income and requires little or no maintenance is

A   Unimproved land.

B   A warehouse with a tenant who is triple-net lease.

C   A single-family residence.

D   A cooperative or condominium unit with a tenant who has a month-to-month lease.

47. The formula for calculating effective gross income is

A   PGI - OI + (V&C) = EGI

B   PGI + OI - (V&C) = EGI

C   PGI + OI + (V&C) = EGI

D   PGI - OI - (V&C) = EGI

48. Variable expenses for an investment property include all of the following EXCEPT

A   Management fees.

B   Payroll.

C   Utilities.

D   Real estate taxes.

49. An investor who wants to buy property, based on an 8 percent cap rate, finds a property that has an NOI of 126,500. How much should the investor be prepared to pay for this property?

A $1,581,250

B $1,375,000

C $1,012,000

D $15,812,500

50. Another term for transfer is

A   alliance

B   alienation

C   avoidance

D   attitude

51. A real estate broker whose office engages in restraints of trade is violating the

A   Civil Rights Act of 1868.

B   Sherman Antitrust Act.

C   General Obligations Law.

D   Law of Agency.

52. When the parties to a transaction agree on the essential terms, what is said to have taken place?

A   A procuring cause of sale.

B   Ratification.

C   Meeting of the minds.

D   Self-dealing.

53. A roofing system that relies on sloping timbers supported by a ridge board and made rigid by interconnecting joists is what kind of roof?

A   Truss.

B   Joist and rafter.

C   Exposed rafter.

D   Gable

54. Jim's neighbor, Ed, regularly uses Jim's driveway to reach his garage. Ed has an easement over Jim's driveway. Jim's property is called

A   the dominant estate

B   an estate

C   a leasehold

D   the servient estate

55. A shared driveway agreement will probably take the form of a(n)

A   voluntary lien

B   affidavit of entitlement

C   easement appurtenant

D   certificate of usage

56. A party wall

A   is located only on a servient estate

B   faces a main road

C   straddles a boundary line

D   is owned by one party

57. The lien with first claim against real estate is

A   a mechanic's lien

B   whatever lien was first recorded

C   a first mortgage

D   the property tax

58. Caveat emptor means

A   Seller beware.

B   Brokers beware.

C   Buyer beware.

D   Client beware.

59. Which of the following is NOT realty?

A   Fee simple estate

B   Freehold estate

C   Timber

D   Life Estate

60. Ownership of which of the following is evidenced by a proprietary lease?

A   Condominium.

B   Cooperative.

C   Time-share.

D   Rent-controlled apartment.

61. Which type of lease only involves a long term lease of land?

A   Net lease.

B   Gross lease.

C   Ground lease.

D   Percentage lease.

62. Impaired physical and mental development in children is a symptom of which of the following environmental hazards?

A   Inhaling asbestos fibers.

B   Presence of leaking underground storage tanks.

C   Lead poisoning.

D   Radon

63. The principle that the worth of a lesser-quality property is enhanced by the presence of a nearby property of greater quality is

A   Proximity.

B   Progression.

C   Competition.

D   Enhancement.

64. In a gross lease, the tenant is required to pay the following in addition to their rental fee:

A   Property Taxes

B   Insurance Fees

C   Maintenance

D   None of the above

65. The Multiple Listing Service is a

A   government program

B   service for cooperating brokerages

C   service for elderly people

D   program for unemployed agents

66. A violation of license law is legally classified as a(n):

A   infraction

B   offense

C   misdemeanor

D   felony

67. Regulation Z does not cover which of the following properties?

A   1 unit family dwelling

B   2 unit family dwelling

C   commercial

D   residential

68. Which of the following is not considered a fiduciary duty?

A   Loyalty

B   Confidentiality

C   Accountability

D   Assumability

69. Which of the following agency relationships, if entered into without a full written disclosure and consent of the parties, is illegal in Wyoming?

A   Open.

B   Dual.

C   Seller.

D   Cooperative.

70. A loan that is paid in 26 half-month payments each year is referred to as what type of mortgage?

A   Amortized.

B   Biweekly.

C   Balloon.

D   Bimonthly.

71. A person who dies without making a will is said to be

A   In probate.

B   Intestate.

C   A testate.

D   A non-legator.

72. The principle that no physical or economic condition remains constant is

A   Progression.

B   Change.

C   Flux.

D   Anticipation.

73. All of the following constitute discriminatory actions on the part of the broker EXCEPT

A   Refusing to deal with an individual because of his or her race.

B   Telling a prospective tenant that there are no units available in an building when in fact units are available.

C   Offering complete relocation services to Catholic while Protestants are left to search the MLS lists unassisted.

D   Showing properties to prospective buyers only in certain, geographic neighborhoods the buyers ask to see.

74. A report of recent sales of similar properties intended to assist an owner in setting a reasonable listing is a

A   Appraisal.

B   Certified market analysis (CMA).

C   Comparative market analysis (CMA)

D   Current market abstract (CMA)

75. A real estate broker whose office engages in restraints of trade is violating the

A   Civil Rights Act of 1868.

B   Sherman Antitrust Act.

C   General Obligations Law.

D   Law of Agency.

Chapter 10

Answers: Practice Test 3

1. C.

A freehold estate is ownership. A lease is the right to occupy, but not ownership.

2. B.

Included with ownership as tenants in common is the right to partition one's interest in the land.

3. B.

If an owner dies intestate and has no living heirs, ownership of the land will revert to the state.

4. B.

The tax due on the sale of the property is capital gains tax.

5. B.

A surety bond is an agreement by an insurance company to be responsible for defaults incurred by an insured party.

6. C.

Radon is a natural gas that may cause lung cancer.

7. B.

CERCLA is administered by the EPA. The law provides a process to identify and hold liable persons responsible for creating hazardous waste.

8. A.

Section 8 housing is a federal housing allowance that provides rent subsidies for low income households.

9. C.

The city planning commission will determine land use through zoning, permits and variances.

10. D.

The city council will vote on laws affecting the local municipality.

11. A.

The certificate of occupancy will allow occupancy of a completed building that has complied with all building codes.

12. B.

Ad valorem means according to value.

13. C.

The local municipality would decide the budget needed to support local government activities.

14. B.

The maximum is $10,000

15. D.

The salesperson is currently working to receive the income.

16. B.

All liens are encumbrances, but not all encumbrances are liens.

17. D.

Transfer taxes are not applicable in the State of Wyoming.

18. B.

An abstract is a summary report and history of all conveyances and encumbrances affecting title to real property.

19. B.

291 days x $12.33 per day = $3587.50

20. B.

These properties are used for a specific use.

21. A.

A variance will permit an exception from the current zoning ordinances.

22. D.

Zoning is police power. A zoning ordinance will regulate land uses.

23.

D.

All would need to give consent for building on wetlands.

24. A.

An appraisal is an educated opinion of value.

25. C.

A comparative market analysis is a comparison of prices of recently sold properties that are similar to the subject property.

26. C.

The appraiser will use a weighted average for the most applicable approach to value.

27. A.

The cost approach is used for special use properties.

28. A.

The Executive Law covers discrimination against race, creed, color, national origin, sexual orientation, and marital status.

29. A.

Fire and hazard insurance cover other hazards such as hail, smoke damage, windstorm etc.

30. C.

Highly protected risk property.

31. D.

If a loan is secured by a property, the lender will require the owner to carry home owners' insurance.

32. A.

The assessed value is the value set on property for taxation purposes.

33. D.

To have a complete transfer of ownership, the deed must be delivered and accepted.

34.

B.

Class 2 is residential with four or more units.

35. C.

Cost is not relevant to the current improvement value.

36. A.

The homeowner's association managers may operate the activities for the complex

37. C.

The owner would have to offer the HOA the unit at the same price before accepting an outside offer.

38. B.

The declaration will include the legal description for the complex and individual units.

39. D.

The bylaws govern the associations activities and powers.

40. D.

A proforma is an estimation of how much income an investment property will generate in the future.

41. C.

The cost of borrowing money and the amount borrowed.

42. B.

The residential property is the least complicated of the listed investment properties.

43. A.

The amount of risk will affect the rate of return. Real estate can be a high-risk investment.

44. D.

Mortgage payments are debt service and not an expense.

45. B.

The UCC is the unification of commercial codes adopted by most states.

46. A.

Land that is unimproved is a type of investment property that produces little or no income and requires little or no maintenance.

47. B.

PGI + OI - (V&C) = EGI is the formula for calculating effective gross income.

48. D.

Real estate taxes are fixed.

49. A.

$126,500/8% = $1,581,250

50. B.

Alienation is another word for transfer.

51. B.

The individual would be violating the Sherman Antitrust Act.

52. C.

A meeting of the minds when term have been agreed to.

53. B.

This would be an example of joist and rafter.

54. D.

The servient estate is the estate that is burdened by the easement

55. C.

An easement appurtenant will run with the land and go to future owners of the property.

56. C.

A party wall is a shared wall between two adjacent parcels of land.

57. D.

Property taxes and special assessments take priority over other liens and will be paid first.

58. C.

This means buyer beware in Latin.

59. C.

Timber is a form of personal property or chattel.

60. B.

In a coop the owner receives a proprietary lease.

61. C.

A ground lease involves a long-term lease of land.

62. C.

A causal connection has been determined between lead poisoning and impaired mental development.

63. B.

This would be the economic principle of progression.

64. D.

In a gross lease the tenant would pay base rent and the landlord would pay for property taxes, insurance and maintenance fees.

65. B.

A service for cooperating brokerages.

66. C.

This is a misdemeanor.

67. C.

Reg Z doesn't apply to commercial real estate.

68. D.

Remember OLDCAR. Assumability is not a fiduciary responsibility.

69. B.

Dual agency requires written consent from seller and buyer.

70. B.

The loan is biweekly.

71. B.

A person that dies without a will is intestate

72. B.

The principle of change states that no economic condition remains constant.

73. D.

This is showing the customer what they want and is not discriminatory.

74. C.

This is a comparative market analysis (CMA).

75. B.

The broker would be in violation of the Sherman Antitrust Act.

Chapter 11

Practice Test 4

1. All of the following are factors that may be used to distinguish an employee from an independent contractor in a real estate office EXCEPT

A   Manner of compensation.

B   Degree of control.

C   Licensed or unlicensed.

D   Written agreement.

2. How is the gross rent multiplier calculated?

A   GRM = Market value/Gross scheduled income

B   GRM = Sales price/ monthly gross rent

C   GRM = Sales price/annual gross income

D   GRM=Gross scheduled income/Market value

3. All of the following would be considered fraudulent acts by a broker EXCEPT

A   Choosing not to disclose certain unpleasant but important facts about property.

B   Telling a prospective buyer certain facts about property that the broker knows are untrue.

C   Deciding not to tell a buyer who is about to make an offer on a house that the neighboring property has been rezoned industrial use.

D   Unintentionally misinforming a buyer by passing on information supplied by the owner.

4. Which of the following is a form of co-ownership that automatically passes to the surviving co-owners when one of the co-owners dies?

A   Tenancy-in-common.

B   Joint tenancy.

C   Corporate ownership.

D   Syndicate ownership.

5. In an adjustable-rate mortgage, the interest rate is raised or lowered, depending on the behavior of a particular

A   Mortgage-backed security.

B   Mortgage index rate.

C   Amortization table.

D   Underwriter.

6. Representing both principal parties in the same transaction without full written disclosure of the fact and the parties' consent is referred to as

A   Undisclosed dual agency.

B   Undisclosed subagency.

C   Subagency-by-ratification.

D   Implied agency.

7. Which of the following correctly expresses the differences between an employee and an independent contractor?

A   Employers have a greater day-to-day control over the work of an independent contractor.

B   Independent contractors are more likely than employees to participate in employer funded health care and pension plans.

C   Brokers are not required to withhold taxes from payments made to independent contractors.

D   Independent contractors are usually compensated on hourly basis rather than simply for performance.

8. How many years must an individual have open, notorious, continuous, uninterrupted, exclusive, and adverse use of another's property to acquire an easement by prescription in Wyoming?

A   7

B   20

C   10

D   25

9. All of the following are government agents in the secondary mortgage market EXCEPT

A   FNMA.

B   HUD.

C   FHLMC.

D   GNMA.

10. A broker formed a real estate business as a sole proprietorship. Which of the following is NOT true of the new business?

A   The broker is entitled to take profits as income.

B   The broker's salary is subject to dual taxation.

C   The tax advantages of the sole proprietorship form are well suited to a small business.

D   The broker's financial liability is unlimited.

11. On a closing statement, items of expense that are incurred, but are not yet payable, are referred to as

A   Incurred items.

B   Accrued items.

C   Liabilities.

D   Prepaid items.

12. In Wyoming the right of election is available to

A   A surviving spouse only.

B   The statutory heirs of a decedent.

C   Any surviving relatives who gives notice within 30 days of the opening of a probate.

D   The decedent's children only.

13. A pro forma is a

A   Report of a property's actual past income - generating performance.

B   Measurement of the degree of investor involvement.

C   Projection of a property's likely performance in the future.

D   Device for calculating the effect of leveraging on accelerated depreciation.

14. A lease that automatically renews for similar succeeding periods creates what type of a tenancy?

A   At will.

B   Periodic.

C   At sufferance.

D   For years.

15. Homes that are produced in a factory and then trucked to a prepared building site to be set onto a foundation are referred to as what type of home?

A   Temporary.

B   Panelized.

C   Modular.

D   Permanent mobile.

16. When the parties to a transaction agree on the essential terms, what is said to have taken place?

A   A procuring cause of sale.

B   Ratification.

C   Meeting of the minds.

D   Self-dealing.

17. The Sherman Act and the Clayton Act are examples of

A   Federal fair employment laws.

B   Wyoming vicarious liability laws.

C Federal antitrust laws.

D Worker's compensation laws.

18. Jones built a garage that was mostly on his property. The northwest corner, however, lay three feet over the property line onto Vell's property. Which of the following best describes the situation?

A Easement in gross.

B Involuntary lien.

C Encroachment.

D Easement appurtenant.

19. Are a salesperson and a broker allowed to form a real estate office partnership in Wyoming?

A Yes, as long as both hold currently active licenses.

B Yes, if they both hold equal interest.

C Yes, if they both register as employee and principal, respectively.

D No.

20. A group of local real estate brokers agree to form an open membership organization to share their listings with one another. Based on these facts alone, is this activity legal?

A No, it is illegal allocation of a market.

B No, it constitutes an illegal restraint of trade.

C No, it is essentially illegal price -fixing.

D Yes, it is essentially a multiple listing service.

21. A real estate broker is usually which type of agent?

A Special.

B   General.

C   Universal.

D   Gratuitous.

22. The Federal Fair Housing Act prohibits discrimination in the sale or rental of residential housing on the basis of all the following EXCEPT

A   Income from public assistance.

B   Race or color.

C   Familial status.

D   Nation of origin.

23. In the rectangular survey system, townships are divided into 36 sections, each one encompassing how many acres?

A   1

B   240

C   360

D   640

24. In an adjustable-rate mortgage, the limitation on the size of any single adjustment during the life of the loan is referred to as a(n)

A   Ceiling.

B   Index.

C   Margin.

D   Cap.

25. The net spendable income generated by an investment is referred to as

A   Capital gain.

B   Depreciation.

C   Cash flow.

D   Leverage.

26. An agent who mixes clients funds with their own personal funds is engaging in

A   Estoppel.

B   Escrow.

C   Commingling.

D   Misrepresentation.

27. An agent who is empowered to represent the principal in a specific range of matters and who may bind the principal to any contract within the scope of the agent 's authority is what kind of agent?

A   Universal.

B   Special.

C   General.

D   Procuring.

28. All of the following are fiduciary duties owed by an agent to a principal EXCEPT

A   Loyalty.

B   Accounting.

C   Obedience.

D   Interest.

29. A mortgage that exceeds the maximum limits set by Fannie Mae and Freddie Mac is what kind of loan?

A   Jumbo.

B   Convertible.

C   Off-index.

D   Premium.

30. Which mortgage clause indicates that when all payments are completed, the mortgagee removes the lien by a satisfaction piece?

A   Contingency clause

B   Acceleration clause

C   Foreclosure clause

D   Defeasance clause

31. Under Wyoming law, whom is required to fully disclose the nature and extent of their agency relationships with whom they have substantive contact?

A   Brokers only.

B   Brokers and salespersons.

C   Sellers only.

D   Buyers, sellers and brokers but not salespersons.

32. All of the following leases are enforceable in Wyoming EXCEPT a(n)

A   Written lease for 15 months.

B   Oral lease for 6 months.

C   Oral lease for 23 months.

D   Acknowledged, recorded three year lease.

33. A person who is in the business of bringing people together for a fee or commission for the purpose of buying, selling, exchanging, or leasing real estate is referred to as a(n)

A   Agent.

B   Broker.

C   Fiduciary.

D   Principal.

34. An amount entered on a closing statement in a person's favor that was paid or to be reimbursed is a(n)

A   Debit.

B   Accrued item.

C   Credit.

D   Caveat.

35. In a life estate, who has a present right to the property if the estate holder dies, while the measuring life is still alive?

A   The measuring life.

B   The estate holder's heirs.

C   The measuring life's heirs.

D   The grantor's heirs.

36. Caveat emptor means

A   Seller beware.

B   Brokers beware.

C   Buyer beware.

D   Client beware.

37. Voluntary medical payments for injuries sustained by guests or resident employees on the insured property are covered by what insurance?

A   Hazard.

B   Liability.

C   Lender's.

D   Local property.

38. Which type of deed provides the most protection for grantees?

A   Bargain and sale.

B   Quitclaim.

C   Covenant.

D   General warranty.

39. Title that is good or clear and reasonably free from risk of lawsuits over defects is

A   Viable.

B   Marketable.

C   Constructive.

D   Actual.

40. Which type of lease only involves a long term lease of land?

A   Net lease.

B   Gross lease.

C   Ground lease.

D   Percentage lease.

41. A broker may compel their independent contractor to

A   Attend office meetings.

B   Earn a specific amount of commissions.

C   Comply with office policy and DOS regulations.

D   Work a specific work week.

42. A mortgage in which the interest rate is raised or lowered during specific periods to reflect the behavior of an index is what type of mortgage?

A   Conventional.

B   Indexed.

C   Fixed-rate.

D   Adjustable-rate.

43. A broker is required to

A   Monitor, train, and supervise the agents under him or her.

B   Pay for agent's continuing education.

C   Make agents purchase E&O insurance to relieve the broker of agent responsibility.

D   Report all infractions to the DOS.

44. A legal proceeding to divide a property that is jointly owned by two or more parties when the cotenants cannot agree on the use or disposition of the property is called

A   Adverse possession.

B   Tacking.

C   Partition.

D   Action to quiet title.

45. A contract in which some term or condition remains to be performed or fulfilled is what type of contract?

A   Executed.

B   Invalid.

C   Unilateral.

D   Executory.

46. The broker who successfully finds a ready, willing, and able buyer for a property is referred to as the

A   Listing broker.

B   Selling broker.

C   Agent.

D   Subagent.

47. Collection and analysis of suspect materials on or near a property is characteristic of which phase of an environmental audit?

A   Phase I

B   Phase II

C   Phase III

D   Phase IV

48. The party who receives property by will is known as the

A   Devisee.

B   Testatee.

C   Bequestor.

D   Grantee.

49. If a foreclosure sale fails to generate sufficient funds to pay off mortgage debt, the mortgagee may seek what kind of judgement?

A   Deficiency.

B   Equity.

C   Satisfaction.

D   Alienation.

50. In Wyoming, a surviving spouse is always entitled to the greater of $50,000, plus what portion of the remainder of the estate?

A   One-quarter.

B   One-half.

C   One-third.

D   Two-thirds.

51. Cash flow + Mortgage amortization + Appreciation + Tax benefits = ?

A   Net operating income.

B   Total return on investment.

C   Operating expenses.

D   Gross expense of investment.

52. A charge levied against a development to help the surrounding community deal with the additional demands for service utilities and schools is a(n)

A   Population adjustment fee (PAF).

B   Impact fee.

C   Special assessment levy.

D   Service maintenance charge (SMC).

53. One point is the equivalent of

A   1/100th of the sales price.

B   1 percent of the loan amount.

C   10 percent of the loan amount.

D   One monthly payment including principle interest, taxes, and insurance.

54. Ownership of which of the following is evidenced by a proprietary lease?

A   Condominium.

B   Cooperative.

C   Time-share.

D   Rent-controlled apartment.

55. The amount added to an adjustable rate mortgage's interest rate to cover the lender's cost is called the

A   Boot.

B   Margin.

C   Cap.

D   Index.

56. What type of prefabricated housing is assembled on-site from segments, such as roof trusses and walls, that are produced elsewhere and shipped to the lot?

A   Panelized housing.

B   Modular homes.

C   Assembly homes.

D   Part-built homes.

57. Substituting a new contract or parties in place of the original is referred to as

A   Release.

B   Novation.

C   Assignment.

D   Implication.

58. Tenants in a mobile home park must be offered leases of at least how long?

A   1 month.

B   6 months.

C   1 year.

D   18 months.

59. A loan in which the principal and the interest is payable in monthly installments over the whole term is what type of loan?

A   ARM.

B   Straight.

C   Amortized.

D   Accelerated.

60. What is the purpose of the real estate license law?

A   To provide the GRI designation to qualified candidates.

B   To certify real estate agents.

C   To protect the public from fraud and set standards of professionalism.

D   To restrict the free operation of legitimate real estate enterprises in the state of Wyoming .

61. The reversion of property to the state of county when a landowner dies interstate and without heirs is

A   Escheat.

B   Laches.

C   Condemnation.

D   Certiorari.

62. Certain disclosure to purchasers of residential property about settlement costs are required by

A   HUD.

B   The Torrens system.

C   FHA.

D   RESPA.

63. The party who makes a will is known at the

A   Devisee.

B   Testator.

C   Legatee.

D   Grantor.

64. Gross rental income minus expenses yields

A   Cash flow.

B   Operating income.

C   Total return on investment.

D   Depreciation.

65. Owners who feel their property taxes are too high may

A   File a tax grievance with the municipality.

B   Refuse to pay it.

C   Take their cases to small claims court.

D   Complain to the building department.

66. The construction of a two-bedroom ranch style brick home in a neighborhood of ranch style brick homes would comply with the principal of

A   Substitution.

B   Competition.

C   Conformity.

D   Anticipation.

67. Compensation in the form of an agreed-upon percentage of the selling price of a property is called a

A   Listing.

B   Market value.

C   Commission.

D   Kickback.

68. A seller is free to employ as many brokers as they wish and must pay a commission only to the broker who successfully produces a qualified buyer in what type of listing?

A   Net.

B   Exclusive-right-to-sell.

C   Open.

D   Unlimited.

69. The standard residential electrical circuit composed of one hot wire, one neutral wire, and a separate ground wire is

A   60-watt.

B   100-volt.

C   110-volt.

D   220-volt.

70. What kind of agent is property manager under most management agreements?

A   Special.

B   General.

C   Limited.

D   Operational.

71. A certificate of title and a Torrens certificate are both

A   Chain of title items.

B   Evidence of title insurance.

C   Evidence of title.

D   Evidence of actual notice.

72. A recorded deed restriction may be enforced by a violator's neighbor by a lawsuit seeking

A   Laches.

B   An injunction.

C   A zoning ordinance.

D   Deed restrictions.

73. A municipality can control development, population density, and building heights through

A   Escheat.

B   Zoning.

C   Laches.

D   Deed restrictions.

74. Rent control regulations apply to buildings with how many units, if built before 1947 and continuously occupied by the current tenant since July 1,1971?

A   Two or more.

B   Three or more.

C   Five or fewer.

D   Any number.

75. Federal law prohibits discrimination against credit applicants on the basis of race, color, religion, national origin, and other factors is what act?

A   RESPA.

B   ECOA.

C   CERCLA.

D   Regulation Z.

Chapter 12

Answers:Practice Test 4

1. C.

Licensing doesn't qualify one as an employee or independent contractor.

2. B.

Gross rent multiplier is used for a one to four unit residential rental property. It is used to calculate an approximate value.

3. D.

The broker acted in good faith.

4. B.

Joint tenancy passes to the co-owners when one of the parties dies.

5. B.

This interest rate is calculated by taking the sum of a benchmark index interest rate and a specified margin.

6. A.

Undisclosed dual agency is illegal.

7. C.

It is up to the independent contractor to pay his/her own taxes.

8. C.

By law it is 10 years.

9. B.

The Department of Housing and Urban Development (HUD) is a U.S. government agency created in 1965 to support community development and home ownership.

10. B.

The broker works as a sole proprietor and therefore is not subject to an additional corporate tax.

11. B.

These are referred to as accrued items on a closing statement.

12. A.

Wyoming provides that the right of election is available to the Spouse.

13. C.

A proforma is a projection of property's performance in the future.

14. B.

This type of lease arrangement is periodic tenancy.

15. C.

These types of houses are modular.

16. C.

When parties to a transaction agree to the essential terms a meeting of the minds has taken place.

17. C.

These are designed to ensure fair trade and competition.

18. C.

This is an example of an encroachment.

19. D.

No, the salesperson would need to be a broker.

20. D.

This is allowed. It is a sharing of listings like MLS.

21. A.

A real estate broker is a special agent.

22. A.

Income from public assistance is not covered under the Federal Fair Housing Act.

23. D.

640 acres.

24. D.

The limitation on the size of any single adjustment during the life of the loan is referred to as a cap.

25. C.

The spendable income from an investment is called cash flow.

26. C.

Commingling of funds is against the law.

27. C.

S/he is a general agent.

28. D.

Remember OLDCAR.

29. A.

A mortgage that exceeds the limits set by FANNIE MAE and FREDDIE MAC is a JUMBO mortage.

30. D.

The defeasance clause is a provision included in a mortgage agreement stating that the lien will be removed when the debt is paid in full.

31. B.

Brokers and salespersons are required to make this agency disclosure.

32. C.

The 23 month oral lease is not enforceable.

33. B.

A broker is in the business of bringing people together for a fee or commission for the purpose of buying, selling, exchanging, or leasing real estate.

34. C.

This is a credit on the Closing Statement.

35. B.

The estate holder's heirs.

36. C.

Latin for 'buyer beware'.

37. B.

This type of insurance is known as liability insurance.

38. D.

The general warranty deed provides the most protection.

39. B.

Marketable title is good or clear and reasonably free from risk of lawsuits over defects.

40. C.

A ground lease typically involves a term of at least 50 years or more.

41. C.

The broker can compel agent to follow office policy and DOS regulations.

42. D.

A mortgage of this type is an adjustable-rate mortgage.

43. A.

A broker is required to monitor, supervise and train the agent under him.

44. C.

This legal proceed is called a partition.

45. D.

This is an executory contract.

46. B.

The selling broker finds a ready, willing, and able buyer for a property.

47. B.

Phase II of an environmental audit involves collection and analysis of suspect materials on or near a property.

48. A.

The party that receives property by will is known as the devisee.

49. A.

The mortgagee may seek a deficiency judgement.

50. C.

The surviving spouse is entitled to 1/3.

51. B.

Cash flow + Mortgage amortization + Appreciation + Tax benefits = Total Return on Investment

52. B.

This is called an impact fee.

53. B.

A point is .01.

54. B.

When you live in a coop you are given a proprietary lease and shares.

55. B.

This amount is referred to as margin.

56. B.

Modular homes are prefabricated elsewhere and then assembled at site.

57. B.

Substituting new parties to a contract is called a novation.

58. C.

Tenants on a mobile home park need a lease of 12 months.

59. C.

This is an amortized loan.

60. C.

This purpose of real estate license law is to protect the public.

61. A.

When a person dies intestate, the reversion of property to the government is called escheat.

62. D.

RESPA requires certain disclosure to purchasers of residential property about settlement costs.

63. B.

A party that makes a will is called a testator.

64. B.

This is operating income.

65. A.

The homeowners may file a grievance with the municipality.

66. C.

This would be in compliance with conformity.

67. C.

This agreed upon percentage is a commission.

68. C.

In an open listing, only the broker that closes will receive a commission.

69. C.

The standard residential circuit is 110-volt.

70. B.

A property manager is a general agent.

71. C.

These are evidence of title.

72. B.

This would be an injunction.

73. B.

A municipality control development, population density, and building heights through zoning.

74. B.

Rent control regulations apply to buildings with three or more units, if built before 1947 and continuously occupied by the current tenant since July 1,1971.

75. B.

The Equal Credit Opportunity Act prohibits discrimination against credit applicants on the basis of race, color, religion, national origin, and other factors.

Glossary

ABANDONMENT — The failure to occupy and use property that may result in a loss of rights.

ABATEMENT OF NUISANCE — Extinction or termination of a nuisance.

ABSOLUTE OWNERSHIP — See FEE SIMPLE ESTATE.

ABSTRACT OF JUDGMENT — A condensation of the essential provisions of a court judgment.

ABSTRACT OF TITLE — A summary or digest of all transfers, conveyances, legal proceedings, and anyother facts relied on as evidence of title, showing continuity of ownership, together with any other elements of record which may impair title.

ABSTRACTION — A method of valuing land. The indicated value of the improvement is deducted from the sale price.

ACCELERATED COST RECOVERY SYSTEM — The system for figuring depreciation (cost recovery) for depreciable real property acquired and placed into service after January 1, 1981. (ACRS)

ACCELERATED DEPRECIATION — A method of cost write-off in which depreciation allowances are greater in the first few years of ownership than in subsequent years. This permits an earlier recovery of capital and a faster tax write-off of an asset.

ACCELERATION CLAUSE — A condition in a real estate financing instrument giving the lender the power to declare all sums owing lender immediately due and payable upon the happening of an event, such as sale of the property, or a delinquency in the repayment of the note.

ACCEPTANCE — The act of agreeing or consenting to the terms of an offer thereby establishing the "meeting of the minds" that is an essential element of a contract.

ACCESS RIGHT — The right of an owner to have ingress and egress to and from owner's property over adjoining property.

ACCESSION — An addition to property through the efforts of man or by natural forces.

ACCRETION — Accession by natural forces, e.g., alluvium.

ACCRUED DEPRECIATION — The difference between the cost of replacement new as of the date of the appraisal and the present appraised value.

ACCRUED ITEMS OF EXPENSE — Those incurred expenses which are not yet payable. The seller's accrued expenses are credited to the purchaser in a closing statement.

ACKNOWLEDGMENT — A formal declaration made before an authorized person, e.g., a notary public, by a person who has executed an instrument stating that the execution was his or her free act. In this state an acknowledgment is the statement by an officer such as a notary that the signatory to the instrument is the person represented to be.

ACOUSTICAL TILE — Blocks of fiber, mineral or metal, with small holes or rough-textured surface to absorb sound, used as covering for interior walls and ceilings.

ACQUISITION — The act or process by which a person procures property.

ACRE — A measure of land equaling 160 square rods, or 4,840 square yards, or 43,560 square feet.

ACTUAL AUTHORITY — Authority expressly given by the principal or given by the law and not denied by the principal.

ACTUAL FRAUD — An act intended to deceive another, e.g., making a false statement, making a promise without intending to perform it, suppressing the truth.

ADDENDUM — Additional pages of material that are added to and become part of a contract.

ADJUSTABLE RATE MORTGAGE (ARM) — A mortgage loan which bears interest at a rate subject to change during the term of the loan, predetermined or otherwise.

ADJUSTMENTS — In appraising, a means by which characteristics of a residential property are regulated by dollar amount or percentage to conform to similar characteristics of another residential property.

ADMINISTRATOR — A person appointed by the probate court to administer the estate of a deceased person who died intestate. (Administratrix, the feminine form.)

ADR — See ALTERNATIVE DISPUTE RESOLUTION.

AD VALOREM — A Latin phrase meaning "according to value." Usually used in connection with real estate taxation.

ADVANCE — Transfer of funds from a lender to a borrower in advance on a loan.

ADVANCE COMMITMENT — The institutional investor's prior agreement to provide long-term financing upon completion of construction; also known as a "take-out" loan commitment.

ADVANCE FEES — A fee paid in advance of any services rendered. Sometimes unlawfully charged in connection with that illegal practice of obtaining a fee in advance for the advertising of property or businesses for sale, with no intent to obtain a buyer, by persons representing themselves as real estate licensees, or representatives of licensed real estate firms.

ADVERSE POSSESSION — A method of acquiring title to real property through possession of the property for a statutory period under certain conditions by a person other than the owner of record.

AFFIANT — One who makes an affidavit or gives evidence.

AFFIDAVIT — A statement or declaration reduced to writing sworn to or affirmed before some officer who has authority to administer an oath or affirmation.

AFFIDAVIT OF TITLE — A statement, in writing, made under oath by seller or grantor, acknowledged

before a Notary Public in which the affiant identifies himself or herself and affiant's marital status certifying that since the examination of title on the contract date there are no judgments, bankruptcies or divorces, no unrecorded deeds, contracts, unpaid repairs or improvements or defects of title known to affiant and that affiant is in possession of the property.

AFFIRM — To confirm, to aver, to ratify, to verify. To make a declaration.

AGENCY — The relationship between principal and the principal's agent which arises out of a contract, either expressed or implied, written or oral, wherein the agent is employed by the principal to do certain acts dealing with a third party.

AGENT — One who acts for and with authority from another called the principal.

AGREEMENT — An exchange of promises, a mutual understanding or arrangement; a contract.

AGREEMENT OF SALE — A written agreement or contract between seller and purchaser in which they reach a "meeting of minds" on the terms and conditions of the sale. The parties concur; are in harmonious opinion.

AIR RIGHTS — The rights in real property to the reasonable use of the air space above the surface of the land.

ALIENATION — The transferring of property to another; the transfer of property and possession of lands, or other things, from one person to another.

ALIENATION CLAUSE — A clause in a contract giving the lender certain rights in the event of a sale or other transfer of mortgaged property.

ALLODIAL TENURE — A real property ownership system where ownership may be complete except for those rights held by government. Allodial is in contrast to feudal tenure.

ALLUVIUM — The gradual increase of the earth on a shore of an ocean or bank of a stream resulting from the action of the water.

ALTA OWNER'S POLICY — An owner's extended coverage policy that provides buyers and owners the same protection the ALTA policy gives to lenders.

ALTA TITLE POLICY — (American Land Title Association) A type of title insurance policy issued by title insurance companies which expands the risks normally insured against under the standard type policy to include unrecorded mechanic's liens; unrecorded physical easements; facts a physical survey would show; water and mineral rights; and rights of parties in possession, such as tenants and buyers under unrecorded instruments.

ALTERNATIVE DISUPUTE RESOLUTION (ADR) — The resolution of disputes by various means including, but not limited to negotiation, mediation, and arbitration.

AMENITIES — Satisfaction of enjoyable living to be derived from a home; conditions of agreeable living or a beneficial influence from the location of improvements, not measured in monetary considerations but rather as tangible and intangible benefits attributable to the property, often causing greater pride in ownership.

AMORTIZATION — The liquidation of a financial obligation on an installment basis; also, recovery over a period of cost or value.

AMORTIZED LOAN — A loan to be repaid, interest and principal, by a series of regular payments that are equal or nearly equal, without any special balloon payment prior to maturity. Also called a Level Payments Loan.

ANNEXATION — The attaching of personal property to land so that the law views it as part of the real property (a fixture). Annexation can be actual or constructive.

ANNUAL PERCENTAGE RATE — The relative cost of credit as determined in accordance with Regulation Z of the Board of Governors of the Federal Reserve System for implementing the Federal Truth in Lending Act.

ANNUITY — A sum of money received at fixed intervals, such as a series of assured equal or nearly equal payments to be made over a period of time, or it may be a lump sum payment to be made in the future. The installment payments due to the landlord under a lease is an annuity. So are the installment payments due to a lender.

ANTICIPATION, PRINCIPLE OF — Affirms that value is created by anticipated benefits to be derived in the future.

APPELLANT — A party appealing a court decision or ruling.

APPRAISAL — An estimate of the value of property resulting from an analysis of facts about the property. An opinion of value.

APPRAISER — One qualified by education, training and experience who is hired to estimate the value of real and personal property based on experience, judgment, facts, and use of formal appraisal processes.

APPROPRIATION OF WATER — The taking, impounding or diversion of water flowing on the public domain from its natural course and the application of the water to some beneficial use personal and exclusive to the appropriator.

APPURTENANCE: That which belongs to something, but not immemorially; all those rights, privileges, and improvements which belong to and pass with the transfer of the property, but which are not necessarily a part of the actual property. Appurtenances to real property pass with the real property to which they are appurtenant, unless a contrary intention is manifested. Typical appurtenances are rights-of-way, easements, water rights, and any property improvements.

APPURTENANT — Belonging to; adjunct; appended or annexed to. For example, the garage is appurtenant to the house, and the common interest in the common elements of a condominium is appurtenant to each apartment. Appurtenant items pass with the land when the property is transferred.

APR — See ANNUAL PERCENTAGE RATE.

ARBITRATION — A neutral third party who listens to each party's position and makes a final binding decision.

ARCHITECTURAL STYLE — Generally the appearance and character of a building's design and construction.

ARTICLES OF INCORPORATION — An instrument setting forth the basic rules and purposes under which a private corporation is formed.

ARTIFICIAL PERSON — Persons created by law; a corporation.

ASSESSED VALUATION — A valuation placed upon a piece of property by a public authority as a basis for levying taxes on the property.

ASSESSMENT — The valuation of property for the purpose of levying a tax or the amount of the tax levied. Also, payments made to a common interest subdivision homeowners- association for maintenance and reserves.

ASSESSOR — The official who has the responsibility of determining assessed values.

ASSIGNMENT — A transfer to another of any property in possession or in action, or of any estate or right therein. A transfer by a person of that person's rights under a contract.

ASSIGNMENT OF RENTS — A provision in a deed of trust (or mortgage) under which the beneficiary may, upon default by the trustor, take possession of the property, collect income from the property and apply it to the loan balance and the costs incurred by the beneficiary.

ASSIGNOR — One who assigns or transfers property.

ASSIGNS, ASSIGNEES — Those to whom property or interests therein shall have been transferred.

ASSUMPTION AGREEMENT — An undertaking or adoption of a debt or obligation primarily resting upon another person.

ASSUMPTION FEE — A lender's charge for changing over and processing new records for a new owner who is assuming an existing loan.

ASSUMPTION OF MORTGAGE — The taking of a title to property by a grantee wherein grantee assumes liability for payment of an existing note secured by a mortgage or deed of trust against the property, becoming a co-guarantor for the payment of a mortgage or deed of trust note.

ATTACHMENT — The process by which real or personal property of a party to a lawsuit is seized and retained in the custody of the court for the purpose of acquiring jurisdiction over the property, to compel an appearance before the court, or to furnish security for a debt or costs arising out of the litigation.

ATTEST — To affirm to be true or genuine; an official act establishing authenticity.

ATTORNEY IN FACT — One who is authorized by another to perform certain acts for another under a power of attorney; power of attorney may be limited to a specific act or acts or be general.

AVULSION — A sudden and perceptible loss of land by the action of water as by a sudden change in the course of a river.

BACKFILL — The replacement of excavated earth into a hole or against a structure.

BALANCE SHEET — A statement of the financial condition of a business at a certain time showing assets, liabilities, and capital.

BALLOON PAYMENT — An installment payment on a promissory note - usually the final one for discharging the debt - which is significantly larger than the other installment payments provided under the terms of the promissory note.

BARGAIN AND SALE DEED — Any deed that recites a consideration and purports to convey the real estate; a bargain and sale deed with a covenant against the grantor's act is one in which the grantor warrants that grantor has done nothing to harm or cloud the title.

BASE AND MERIDIAN — Imaginary lines used by surveyors to find and describe the location of private or public lands. In government surveys, a base line runs due east and west, meridians run due north and south, and are used to establish township boundaries.

BASIS — (1) Cost Basis—The dollar amount assigned to property at the time of acquisition under provisions of the Internal Revenue Code for the purpose of determining gain, loss and depreciation in calculating the income tax to be paid upon the sale or exchange of the property. (2) Adjusted Cost Basis—The cost basis after the application of certain additions for improvements, etc., and deductions for depreciation, etc.

BEARING WALL — A wall or partition which supports a part of a building, usually a roof or floor above.

BENCH MARK — A monument used to establish the elevation of the point, usually relative to Mean Sea Level, but often to some local datum.

BENEFICIARY — (1) One entitled to the benefit of a trust; (2) One who receives profit from an estate, the title of which is vested in a trustee; (3) The lender on the security of a note and deed of trust.

BEQUEATH — To give or hand down by will; to leave by will.

BEQUEST — Personal property given by the terms of a will.

BETTERMENT — An improvement upon property which increases the property value and is considered as a capital asset as distinguished from repairs or replacements where the original character or cost is unchanged.

BILL OF SALE — A written instrument given to pass title of personal property from vendor to the vendee.

BINDER — An agreement to consider a down payment for the purchase of real estate as evidence of good faith on the part of the purchaser. Also, a notation of coverage on an insurance policy, issued by an agent, and given to the insured prior to issuing of the policy.

BLANKET MORTGAGE — A single mortgage which covers more than one piece of real property.

BLIGHTED AREA — A district affected by detrimental influences of such extent or quantity that real property values have seriously declined as a result of adverse land use and/or destructive economic forces; characterized by rapidly depreciating buildings, retrogression and no recognizable prospects for improvement. However, renewal programs and changes in use may lead to resurgence of such areas.

BLOCKBUSTING — The practice on the part of unscrupulous speculators or real estate agents of inducing panic selling of homes at prices below market value, especially by exploiting the prejudices of property owners in neighborhoods in which the racial make-up is changing or appears to be on the verge of changing.

BONA FIDE — In good faith; without fraud or deceit; authentic.

BOND — Written evidence of an obligation given by a corporation or government entity. A surety instrument.

BOOK VALUE — The current value for accounting purposes of an asset expressed as original cost plus capital additions minus accumulated depreciation.

BREACH — The breaking of a law, or failure of duty, either by omission or commission.

BROKER — A person employed for a fee by another to carry on any of the activities listed in the license law definition of a broker.

BROKER-SALESPERSON RELATIONSHIP AGREEMENT — A written agreement required by the regulations of the Real Estate Commissioner setting forth the material aspects of the relationship between a real estate broker and each salesperson and broker performing licensed activities in the name of the supervising broker.

B.T.U. — British thermal unit. The quantity of heat required to raise the temperature of one pound of water one degree Fahrenheit.

BUILDING CODE — A systematic regulation of construction of buildings within a municipality established by ordinance or law.

BUILDING LINE — A line set by law a certain distance from a street line in front of which an owner cannot build on owner's lot. A setback line.

BUILDING, MARKET VALUE OF — The sum of money which the presence of that structure adds to or subtracts from the value of the land it occupies. Land valued on the basis of highest and best use.

BUILDING RESTRICTIONS — Zoning, regulatory requirements or provisions in a deed limiting the type, size and use of a building.

BUNDLE OF RIGHTS — All of the legal rights incident to ownership of property including rights of use, possession, encumbering and disposition.

BUREAU OF LAND MANAGEMENT — A federal bureau within the Department of the Interior which manages and controls certain lands owned by the United States.

BUSINESS OPPORTUNITY — The assets for an existing business enterprise including its goodwill. As used in the Real Estate Law, the term includes "the sale or lease of the business and goodwill of an existing business enterprise or opportunity."

BUYER'S MARKET — The condition which exists when a buyer is in a more commanding position as to price and terms because real property offered for sale is in plentiful supply in relation to demand.

BYLAWS — Rules for the conduct of the internal affairs of corporations and other organizations.

CC&Rs — Covenants, conditions and restrictions. The basic rules establishing the rights and obligations of owners (and their successors in interest) of real property within a subdivision or other tract of land in relation to other owners within the same subdivision or tract and in relation to an association of owners organized for the purpose of operating and maintaining property commonly owned by the individual owners.

CCIM — Certified Commercial Investment Member.

CPM© — Certified Property Manager, a designation of the Institute of Real Estate Management.

CAPACITY — The legal ability to perform some act, such as enter into a contract or execute a deed or will.

CAPITAL ASSETS — Assets of a permanent nature used in the production of an income, such as land, buildings, machinery and equipment, etc. Under income tax law, it is usually distinguishable from "inventory" which comprises assets held for sale to customers in ordinary course of the taxpayer's trade or business.

CAPITAL GAIN — At resale of a capital item, the amount by which the net sale proceeds exceed the adjusted cost basis (book value). Used for income tax computations. Gains are called short or long term based upon length of holding period after acquisition. Usually taxed at lower rates than ordinary income.

CAPITALIZATION — In appraising, determining value of property by considering net income and percentage of reasonable return on the investment. The value of an income property is determined by dividing annual net income by the Capitalization Rate.

CAPITALIZATION RATE — The rate of interest which is considered a reasonable return on the investment, and used in the process of determining value based upon net income. It may also be described as the yield rate that is necessary to attract the money of the average investor to a particular kind of investment. In the case of land improvements which depreciate, to this yield rate is added a factor to take into consideration the annual amortization factor necessary to recapture the initial investment in improvements. This amortization factor can be determined in various ways — (1) straight-line depreciation method, (2) Inwood Tables and (3) Hoskold Tables. (To explore this subject in greater depth, the student should refer to current real estate appraisal texts.)

CARRYBACK LOAN — The extension of credit from the seller to the buyer to finance the purchase of the property, accepting a deed of trust or mortgage instead of cash. Sometimes called a purchase money loan.

CASEMENT WINDOWS — Frames of wood or metal which swing outward.

CASH FLOW — The net income generated by a property before depreciation and other noncash expenses.

CAVEAT EMPTOR — Let the buyer beware. The buyer must examine the goods or property and buy at his or her own risk, absent misrepresentation.

CERTIFICATE OF ELIGIBILITY — Issued by Department of Veterans Affairs - evidence of individual's eligibility to obtain VA loan.

CERTIFICATE OF REASONABLE VALUE (CRV) — The Federal VA appraisal commitment of property value.

CERTIFICATE OF TAXES DUE — A written statement or guaranty of the condition of the taxes on a certain property made by the County Treasurer of the county wherein the property is located. Any loss resulting to any person from an error in a tax certificate shall be paid by the county which such treasurer represents.

CERTIFICATE OF TITLE — A written opinion by an attorney that ownership of the particular parcel of land is as stated in the certificate.

CHAIN — A unit of measurement used by surveyors. A chain consists of 100 links equal to 66 feet.

CHAIN OF TITLE — A history of conveyances and encumbrances affecting the title from the time then original patent was granted, or as far back as records are available, used to determine how title came to be vested in current owner.

CHANGE, PRINCIPLE OF — Holds that it is the future, not the past, which is of prime importance in estimating value. Change is largely result of cause and effect.

CHARACTERISTICS — Distinguishing features of a (residential) property.

CHATTEL MORTGAGE — A claim on personal property (instead of real property) used to secure or guarantee a promissory note. (See definition of Security Agreement and Security Interest.)

CHATTEL REAL — An estate related to real estate, such as a lease on real property.

CHATTEL —Personal property.

CHOSE IN ACTION — A personal right to something not presently in the owner's possession, but recoverable by a legal action for possession.

CIRCUIT BREAKER — (l) An electrical device which automatically interrupts an electric circuit when an overload occurs; may be used instead of a fuse to protect each circuit and can be reset. (2) In property taxation, a method for granting property tax relief to the elderly and disadvantaged qualified taxpayers by rebate, tax credits or cash payments. Usually limited to homeowners and renters.

CLOSING — (l) Process by which all the parties to a real estate transaction conclude the details of a sale or mortgage. The process includes the signing and transfer of documents and distribution of funds. (2) Condition in description of real property by courses and distances at the boundary lines where the lines meet to include all the tract of land.

CLOSING COSTS — The miscellaneous expenses buyers and sellers normally incur in the transfer of ownership of real property over and above the cost of the property.

CLOSING STATEMENT — An accounting of funds made to the buyer and seller separately. Required by law to be made at the completion of every real estate transaction.

CLOUD ON TITLE — A claim, encumbrance or condition which impairs the title to real property until disproved or eliminated as for example through a quitclaim deed or a quiet title legal action.

CODE OF ETHICS — A set of rules and principles expressing a standard of accepted conduct for a professional group and governing the relationship of members to each other and to the organization.

COLLATERAL — Marketable real or personal property which a borrower pledges as security for a loan. In mortgage transactions, specific land is the collateral.

COLLATERAL SECURITY — A separate obligation attached to contract to guarantee its performance; the transfer of property or of other contracts, or valuables, to insure the performance of a principal agreement.

COLLUSION — An agreement between two or more persons to defraud another of rights by the forms of law, or to obtain an object forbidden by law.

COLOR OF TITLE — That which appears to be good title but which is not title in fact.

COMMERCIAL ACRE — A term applied to the remainder of an acre of newly subdivided land after the area devoted to streets, sidewalks and curbs, etc., has been deducted from the acre.

COMMERCIAL LOAN — A personal loan from a commercial bank, usually unsecured and short term, for other than mortgage purposes.

COMMERCIAL PAPER — Negotiable instruments such as promissory notes, letters of credit and bills of lading. Instruments developed under the law of merchant.

COMMINGLING — The illegal mixing of personal funds with money held in trust on behalf of a client.

COMMISSION — An agent's compensation for performing the duties of the agency; in real estate practice, a percentage of the selling price of property, percentage of rentals, etc. A fee for services.

COMMITMENT — A pledge or a promise or firm agreement to do something in the future, such as a loan company giving a written commitment with specific terms of mortgage loan it will make.

COMMON AREA — An entire common interest subdivision except the separate interests therein.

COMMON INTEREST SUBDIVISION — Subdivided lands which include a separate interest in real property combined with an interest in common with other owners. The interest in common may be through membership in an association. Examples are condominiums and stock cooperatives.

COMMON LAW — The body of law that grew from customs and practices developed and used in England.

COMMON STOCK — That class of corporate stock to which there is ordinarily attached no preference with respect to the receipt of dividends or the distribution of assets on corporate dissolution.

COMMUNITY PROPERTY — Property acquired by husband and/or wife during a marriage when not acquired as the separate property of either spouse. Each spouse has equal rights of management, alienation and testamentary disposition of community property.

COMPACTION — Whenever extra soil is added to a lot to fill in low places or to raise the level of the lot, the added soil is often too loose and soft to sustain the weight of the buildings. Therefore, it is necessary to compact the added soil so that it will carry the weight of buildings without the danger of their tilting, settling or cracking.

COMPARABLE SALES — Sales which have similar characteristics as the subject property and are used for analysis in the appraisal process. Commonly called "comparables", they are recent selling prices of properties similarly situated in a similar market.

COMPARISON APPROACH — A real estate comparison method which compares a given property with similar or comparable surrounding properties; also called market comparison.

COMPETENT — Legally qualified.

COMPETITION, PRINCIPLE OF — Holds that profits tend to breed competition and excess profits tend to breed ruinous completion.

COMPOUND INTEREST — Interest paid on original principal and also on the accrued and unpaid interest which has accumulated as the debt matures.

CONCLUSION — The final estimate of value, realized from facts, data, experience and judgment, set out in an appraisal. Appraiser's certified conclusion.

CONDEMNATION — The act of taking private property for public use by a political subdivision upon payment to owner of just compensation. Declaration that a structure is unfit for use.

CONDITION — In contracts, a future and uncertain event which must happen to create an obligation or which extinguishes an existent obligation. In conveyances of real property conditions in the conveyance may cause an interest to be vested or defeated.

CONDITION PRECEDENT — A qualification of a contract or transfer of property, providing that unless and until a given event occurs, the full effect of a contract or transfer will not take place.

CONDITION SUBSEQUENT — A condition attached to an already-vested estate or to a contract whereby the estate is defeated or the contract extinguished through the failure or non-performance of the condition.

CONDITIONAL COMMITMENT — A commitment of a definite loan amount for some future unknown purchaser of satisfactory credit standing.

CONDITIONAL SALE CONTRACT — A contract for the sale of property stating that delivery is to be made to the buyer, title to remain vested in the seller until the conditions of the contract have been fulfilled.

CONDOMINIUM — An estate in real property wherein there is an undivided interest in common in a portion of real property coupled with a separate interest in space called a unit, the boundaries of which are described on a recorded final map, parcel map or condominium plan. The areas within the boundaries may be filled with air, earth, or water or any combination and need not be attached to land except by easements for access and support.

CONDOMINIUM DECLARATION — The document which establishes a condominium and describes the property rights of the unit owners.

CONFESSION OF JUDGMENT — An entry of judgment upon the debtor's voluntary admission or confession.

CONFIRMATION OF SALE — A court approval of the sale of property by an executor, administrator, guardian or conservator.

CONFISCATION — The seizing of property without compensation.

CONFORMITY, PRINCIPLE OF — Holds that the maximum of value is realized when a reasonable degree of homogeneity of improvements is present. Use conformity is desirable, creating and maintaining higher values.

CONSERVATION — The process of utilizing resources in such a manner which minimizes their depletion.

CONSIDERATION — Anything given or promised by a party to induce another to enter into a contract, e.g., personal services or even love and affection. It may be a benefit conferred upon one party or a detriment suffered by the other.

CONSTANT — The percentage which, when applied directly to the face value of a debt, develops the annual amount of money necessary to pay a specified net rate of interest on the reducing balance and to liquidate the debt in a specified time period. For example, a 6% loan with a 20 year amortization has a constant of approximately 8 1/2%. Thus, a $10,000 loan amortized over 20 years requires an annual payment of approximately $850.00.

CONSTRUCTION LOAN — A loan made to finance the actual construction or improvement on land. Funds are usually dispersed in increments as the construction progresses.

CONSTRUCTIVE EVICTION — Breach of a covenant of warranty or quiet enjoyment, e.g., the inability of a lessee to obtain possession because of a paramount defect in title or a condition making occupancy hazardous.

CONSTRUCTIVE FRAUD — A breach of duty, as by a person in a fiduciary capacity, without an actual fraudulent intent, which gains an advantage to the person at fault by misleading another to the other's prejudice. Any act of omission declared by law to be fraudulent, without respect to actual fraud.

CONSTRUCTIVE NOTICE — Notice of the condition of title to real property given by the official records of a government entity which does not require actual knowledge of the information.

CONTIGUOUS — In close proximity.

CONTOUR — The surface configuration of land. Shown on maps as a line through points of equal elevation.

CONTRACT — An agreement to do or not to do a certain thing. It must have four essential elements —parties capable of contracting, consent of the parties, a lawful object, and consideration. A contract for sale of real property must also be in writing and signed by the party or parties to be charged with performance.

CONTRACT, BILATERAL — A contract in which each party promises to do something.

CONTRACT, EXECUTED — 1) A contract in which both parties have completely performed their contractual obligations. 2) A signed contract.

CONTRACT, EXECUTORY — A contract in which one or both parties have not yet completed performance of their obligations.

CONTRACT, EXPRESS — A contract that has been put into words, either spoken or written.

CONTRACT, IMPLIED — An agreement that has not been put into words, but is implied by the actions of the parties.

CONTRACT, UNILATERAL — When one party promises to do something if the other party performs a certain act, but the other party does not promise to perform it; the contract is formed only if the other party does perform the requested act.

CONTRIBUTION, PRINCIPLE OF — A component part of a property is valued in proportion to its contribution to the value of the whole. Holds that maximum values are achieved when the improvements on a site produce the highest (net) return, commensurate with the investment.

CONVENTIONAL MORTGAGE — A mortgage securing a loan made by investors without governmental underwriting, i.e., which is not FHA insured or VA guaranteed. The type customarily made by a bank or savings and loan association.

CONVERSION — (1) Change from one legal form or use to another, as converting an apartment building to condominium use. (2) The unlawful appropriation of another's property, as in the conversion of trust funds.

CONVEYANCE — An instrument in writing used to transfer (convey) title to property from one person to another, such as a deed or a trust deed.

COOPERATIVE (apartment) — An apartment building, owned by a corporation and in which tenancy in an apartment unit is obtained by purchase of shares of the stock of the corporation and where the owner of such shares is entitled to occupy a specific apartment in the building.
CORNER INFLUENCE

TABLE — A statistical table that may be used to estimate the added value of a corner lot.

CORPORATION — An entity established and treated by law as an individual or unit with rights and liabilities, or both, distinct and apart from those of the persons composing it. A corporation is a creature of law having certain powers and duties of a natural person. Being created by law it may continue for any length of time the law prescribes.

CORPOREAL RIGHTS — Possessory rights in real property.

CORRECTION LINES — A system for compensating inaccuracies in the Government Rectangular Survey System due to the curvature of the earth. Every fourth township line, 24 mile intervals, is used as a correction line on which the intervals between the north and south range lines are remeasured and corrected to a full 6 miles.

CORRELATION — A step in the appraisal process involving the interpretation of data derived from the three approaches to value (cost, market and income) leading to a single determination of value. Also frequently referred to as "reconciliation."

CO-SIGNER — A second party who signs a promissory note together with the primary borrower.

COST APPROACH — One of three methods in the appraisal process. An analysis in which a value estimate of a property is derived by estimating the replacement cost of the improvements, deducting there from the estimated accrued depreciation, then adding the market value of the land.

COTENANCY — Ownership of an interest in a particular parcel of land by more than one person; e.g. tenancy in common, joint tenancy.

COUNTER OFFER — A response to an offer to enter into a contract, changing some of the terms of the terms of the original offer. A counter offer is a rejection of the offer (not a form of acceptance), and does not create a binding contract unless accepted by the original offeror.

COVENANT — An agreement or promise to do or not to do a particular act such as a promise to build a house of a particular architectural style or to use or not use property in a certain way.

CRAWL HOLE — Exterior or interior opening permitting access underneath building, as required by building codes.

CRE — Counselor of Real Estate, Member of American Society of Real Estate Counselors.

CREDIT — A bookkeeping entry on the right side of an account, recording the reduction or elimination of an asset or an expense, or the creation of or addition to a liability or item of equity or revenue.

CURABLE DEPRECIATION — Items of physical deterioration and functional obsolescence which are customarily repaired or replaced by a prudent property owner.

CURRENT INDEX — With regard to an adjustable rate mortgage, the current value of a recognized index as calculated and published nationally or regionally. The current index value changes periodically and is used in calculating the new note rate as of each rate adjustment date.

CURTAIL SCHEDULE — A listing of the amounts by which the principal sum of an obligation is to be reduced by partial payments and of the dates when each payment will become payable.

DAMAGES — The indemnity recoverable by a person who has sustained an injury, either in his or her person, property, or relative rights, through the act or default of another. Loss sustained or harm done to a person or property.

DATA PLANT — An appraiser's file of information on real estate.

DEBENTURE — Bonds issued without security, an obligation not secured by a specific lien on property.

DEBIT — A bookkeeping entry on the left side of an account, recording the creation of or addition to an asset or an expense, or the reduction or elimination of a liability or item of equity or revenue.

DEBT — That which is due from one person or another; obligation, liability.

DEBTOR — A person who is in debt; the one owing money to another.

DECLINING BALANCE DEPRECIATION — A method of accelerated depreciation allowed by the IRS in certain circumstances. Double Declining Balance Depreciation is its most common form and is computed by using double the rate used for straight line depreciation.

DECREE OF FORECLOSURE — Decree by a court ordering the sale of mortgaged property and the payment of the debt owing to the lender out of the proceeds.

DEDICATION — The giving of land by its owner to a public use and the acceptance for such use by authorized officials on behalf of the public.

DEED — Written instrument which when properly executed and delivered conveys title to real property from one person (grantor) to another (grantee).

DEED IN LIEU OF FORECLOSURE — A deed to real property accepted by a lender from a defaulting borrower to avoid the necessity of foreclosure proceedings by the lender.

DEED RESTRICTIONS — Limitations in the deed to a property that dictate certain uses that may or may not be made of the property.

DEFAULT — Failure to fulfill a duty or promise or to discharge an obligation; omission or failure to perform any act.

DEFEASANCE CLAUSE — The clause in a mortgage that gives the mortgagor the right to redeem mortgagor's property upon the payment of mortgagor's obligations to the mortgagee.

DEFEASIBLE FEE — Sometimes called a base fee or qualified fee; a fee simple absolute interest in land that is capable of being defeated or terminated upon the happening of a specified event.

DEFENDANT — A person against whom legal action is initiated for the purpose of obtaining criminal sanctions (criminal defendant) or damages or other appropriate judicial relief (civil defendant) .

DEFERRED MAINTENANCE — Existing but unfulfilled requirements for repairs and rehabilitation. Postponed or delayed maintenance causing decline in a building's physical condition.

DEFERRED PAYMENT OPTIONS — The privilege of deferring income payments to take advantage of statutes affording tax benefits.

DEFICIENCY JUDGMENT — A judgment given by a court when the value of security pledged for a loan is insufficient to pay off the debt of the defaulting borrower.

DELEGATION OF POWERS — The conferring by an agent upon another of all or certain of the powers that have been conferred upon the agent by the principal.

DEPOSIT RECEIPT — A term used by the real estate industry to describe the written offer to purchase real property upon stated term and conditions, accompanied by a deposit toward the purchase price, which becomes the contract for the sale of the property upon acceptance by the owner.

DEPRECIATION — Loss of value of property brought about by age, physical deterioration or functional oreconomic obsolescence. The term is also used in accounting to identify the amount of the decrease in value of an asset that is allowed in computing the value of the property for tax purposes.

DEPTH TABLE — A statistical table that may be used to estimate the value of the added depth of a lot.

DESIST AND REFRAIN ORDER — An order directing a person to stop from committing an act in violation of the Real Estate Law.

DETERMINABLE FEE — An estate which may end on the happening of an event that may or may not occur.

DEVISE — A gift or disposal of real property by last will and testament.

DEVISEE — One who receives a gift of real property by will.

DEVISOR — One who disposes of real property by will.

DIRECTIONAL GROWTH — The location or direction toward which the residential sections of a city are destined or determined to grow.

DISCOUNT — To sell a promissory note before maturity at a price less than the outstanding principal balance of the note at the time of sale. Also an amount deducted in advance by the lender from the nominal principal of a loan as part of the cost to the borrower of obtaining the loan.

DISCOUNT POINTS — The amount of money the borrower or seller must pay the lender to get a mortgage at a stated interest rate. This amount is equal to the difference between the principal balance on the note and the lesser amount which a purchaser of the note would pay the original lender for it under market conditions. A point equals one percent of the loan.

DISCRETIONARY POWERS OF AGENCY — Those powers conferred upon an agent by the principal which empower the agent in certain circumstances to make decisions based on the agent's own judgment.

DISINTERMEDIATION — The relatively sudden withdrawal of substantial sums of money savers have deposited with savings and loan associations, commercial banks, and mutual savings banks. This term can also be considered to include life insurance policy purchasers borrowing against the value of their policies. The essence of this phenomenon is financial intermediaries losing within a short period of time billions of dollars as owners of funds held by those institutional lenders exercise their prerogative of taking them out of the hands of these financial institutions.

DISPOSABLE INCOME — The after-tax income a household receives to spend on personal consumption.

DISPOSSESS — To deprive one of the use of real estate.

DOCUMENTARY TRANSFER TAX — A state enabling act allows a county to adopt a documentary transfer tax to apply on all transfers of real property located in the county. Notice of payment is entered on face of the deed or on a separate paper filed with the deed.

DOCUMENTS — Legal instruments such as mortgages, contracts, deeds, options, wills, bills of sale, etc.

DONEE — A person who receives a gift.

DONOR — A person who makes a gift.

DRAW — Usually applies to construction loans when disbursement of a portion of the mortgage is made in advance, as improvements to the property are made.

DUAL AGENCY — An agency relationship in which the agent acts concurrently for both of the principals in a transaction.

DUE ON SALE CLAUSE — An acceleration clause granting the lender the right to demand full payment of the mortgage upon a sale of the property.

DURESS — Unlawful constraint exercised upon a person whereby he or she is forced to do some act against his or her will.

EARNEST MONEY — Down payment made by a purchaser of real estate as evidence of good faith. A deposit or partial payment.

EASEMENT — A right, privilege or interest limited to a specific purpose which one party has in the land of another.

ECONOMIC LIFE — The period over which a property will yield a return on the investment over and above the economic or ground rent due to land.

ECONOMIC OBSOLESCENCE — A loss in value due to factors away from the subject property but adversely affecting the value of the subject property.

ECONOMIC RENT — The reasonable rental expectancy if the property were available for renting at the time of its valuation.

EFFECTIVE AGE OF IMPROVEMENT — The number of years of age that is indicated by the condition of the structure, distinct from chronological age.

EFFECTIVE DATE OF VALUE — The specific day the conclusion of value applies.

EFFECTIVE INTEREST RATE — The percentage of interest that is actually being paid by the borrower for the use of the money, distinct from nominal interest.

EMBLEMENTS — The crops and other annual plantings considered to be personal property of the cultivator.

EMINENT DOMAIN — The right of the government to acquire property for necessary public or quasi-public use by condition; the owner must be fairly compensated and the right of the private citizen to get paid is spelled out in the 5th Amendment to the United States Constitution.

ENCROACHMENT — An unlawful intrusion onto another's adjacent property by improvements to real property, e.g. a swimming pool built across a property line.

ENCUMBRANCE — Anything which affects or limits the fee simple title to or value of property, e.g., mortgages or easements.

EQUITY — The interest or value which an owner has in real estate over and above the liens against it. Branch of remedial justice by and through which relief is afforded to suitors in courts of equity.

EQUITY BUILD-UP — The increase of owner's equity in property due to mortgage principal reduction and value appreciation.

EQUITY PARTICIPATION — A mortgage transaction in which the lender, in addition to receiving a fixed rate of interest on the loan acquires an interest in the borrower's real property, and shares in the profits derived from the real property.

EQUITY OF REDEMPTION — The right to redeem property during the foreclosure period, such as a mortgagor's right to redeem within either 3 months or 1 year as may be permitted after foreclosure sale.

EROSION — The wearing away of land by the act of water, wind or glacial ice.

ESCALATION — The right reserved by the lender to increase the amount of the payments and/or interest upon the happening of a certain event.

ESCALATOR CLAUSE — A clause in a contract providing for the upward or downward adjustment of certain items to cover specified contingencies, usually tied to some index or event. Often used in long term leases to provide for rent adjustments, to cover tax and maintenance increases.

ESCHEAT — The reverting of property to the State when heirs capable of inheriting are lacking.

ESCROW — The deposit of instruments and/or funds with instructions with a third neutral party to carry out the provisions of an agreement or contract.

ESCROW AGENT — The neutral third party holding funds or something of value in trust for another or others.

ESTATE — As applied to real estate, the term signifies the quantity of interest, share, right, equity, of which riches or fortune may consist in real property. The degree, quantity, nature and extent of interest which a person has in real property.

ESTATE OF INHERITANCE — An estate which may descend to heirs. All freehold estates are estates of inheritance, except estates for life.

ESTATE FOR LIFE — A possessory, freehold estate in land held by a person only for the duration of his or her life or the life or lives of another.

ESTATE FROM PERIOD TO PERIOD — An interest in land where there is no definite termination date but the rental period is fixed at a certain sum per week, month, or year. Also called a periodic tenancy.

ESTATE AT SUFFERANCE — An estate arising when the tenant wrongfully holds over after the expiration of the term. The landlord has the choice of evicting the tenant as a trespasser or accepting such tenant for a similar term and under the conditions of the tenant's previous holding. Also called a tenancy at sufferance.

ESTATE AT WILL — The occupation of lands and tenements by a tenant for an indefinite period, terminable by one or both parties.

ESTATE FOR YEARS — An interest in lands by virtue of a contract for the possession of them for a definite and limited period of time. May be for a year or less. A lease may be said to be an estate for years.

ESTIMATE — A preliminary opinion of value. Appraise, set a value.

ESTIMATED REMAINING LIFE — The period of time (years) it takes for the improvements to become valueless.

ESTOPPEL — A legal theory under which a person is barred from asserting or denying a fact because of the person's previous acts or words.

ETHICS — That branch of moral science, idealism, justness, and fairness, which treats of the duties which a member of a profession or craft owes to the public, client or partner, and to professional brethren or members. Accepted standards of right and wrong. Moral conduct, behavior or duty.

ET UX — Abbreviation for "et uxor." Means "and wife."

EVICTION — Dispossession by process of law. The act of depriving a person of the possession of lands in pursuance of the judgment of a court.

EXCEPTIONS — Matters affecting title to a particular parcel of real property which are included from coverage of a title insurance policy.

EXCHANGE — A means of trading equities in two or more real properties, treated as a single transaction through a single escrow.

EXCLUSION — General matters affecting title to real property excluded from coverage of a title insurance policy.

EXCLUSIVE AGENCY LISTING — A listing agreement employing a broker as the sole agent for the seller of real property under the terms of which the broker is entitled to a commission if the property is sold through any other broker, but not if a sale is negotiated by the owner without the services of an agent.

EXCLUSIVE RIGHT TO SELL LISTING — A listing agreement employing a broker to act as agent for the seller of real property under the terms of which the broker is entitled to a commission if the property is sold during the duration of the listing through another broker or by the owner without the services of an agent.

EXECUTE — To complete, to make, to perform, to do, to follow out; to execute a deed, to make a deed, including especially signing, sealing and delivery; to execute a contract is to perform the contract, to follow out to the end, to complete.

EXECUTOR — A man named in a will to carry out its provisions as to the disposition of the estate of a deceased person. (A woman is executrix.)

EXECUTORY CONTRACT — A contract in which something remains to be done by one or both of the parties.

EXPENSES — Certain items which appear on a closing statement in connection with a real estate sale.

FACADE — The front of a building, often used to refer to a false front and as a metaphor.

FAIR MARKET VALUE — This is the amount of money that would be paid for a property offered on the open market for a reasonable period of time with both buyer and seller knowing all the uses to which the property could be put and with neither party being under pressure to buy or sell.

FANNIE MAE — An acronymic nickname for Federal National Mortgage Association (FNMA).

FARMERS HOME ADMINISTRATION — An agency of the Department of Agriculture. Primary responsibility is to provide financial assistance for farmers and others living in rural areas where financing is not available on reasonable terms from private sources.

FEDERAL DEPOSIT INSURANCE CORPORATION — (FDIC) Agency of the federal government which insures deposits at commercial banks, savings banks and savings and loans.

FEDERAL HOME LOAN MORTGAGE CORPORATION — An independent stock company which creates a secondary market in conventional residential loans and in FHA and VA loans by purchasing mortgages.

FEDERAL HOUSING ADMINISTRATION — (FHA) An agency of the federal government that insures private mortgage loans for financing of new and existing homes and home repairs.

FEDERAL LAND BANK SYSTEM — Federal government agency making long term loans to farmers.

FEDERAL NATIONAL MORTGAGE ASSOCIATION — (FNMA) "**Fannie Mae**" a quasi-public agency converted into a private corporation whose primary function is to buy and sell **FHA** and **VA** mortgages in the secondary market.

FEDERAL RESERVE SYSTEM — The federal banking system of the United States under the control of central board of governors (Federal Reserve Board) involving a central bank in each of twelve geographical districts with broad powers in controlling credit and the amount of money in circulation.

FEE — An estate of inheritance in real property.

FEE SIMPLE — The maximum possible estate in land in which the owner holds unconditional power of disposition; an estate freely transferable and inheritable.

FEE SIMPLE DEFEASIBLE — An estate in fee subject to the occurrence of a condition subsequent whereby the estate may be terminated.

FEE SIMPLE ESTATE — The greatest interest that one can have in real property. An estate that is unqualified, of indefinite duration, freely transferable and inheritable.

FEUDAL TENURE — A real property ownership system in which ownership rests with a sovereign who may grant lesser interests in return for service or loyalty. This is in contrast to allodial tenure.

FIDELITY BOND — A security posted for the discharge of an obligation of personal services.

FIDUCIARY — A person in a position of trust and confidence, as between principal and broker; broker as fiduciary owes certain loyalty which cannot be breached under the rules of agency.

FIDUCIARY DUTY — That duty owed by an agent to act in the highest good faith toward the principal and not to obtain any advantage over the latter by the slightest misrepresentation, concealment, duress or pressure.

FILTERING — The process whereby higher-priced properties become available to lower income buyers.

FINANCIAL INTERMEDIARY — Financial institutions such as commercial banks, savings and loan associations, mutual savings banks and life insurance companies which receive relatively small sums of money from the public and invest them in the form of large sums. A considerable portion of these funds are loaned on real estate.

FINANCING PROCESS — The systematic 5 step procedure followed by major institutional lenders in analyzing a proposed loan, which includes — filing of application by a borrower; lender's analysis of borrower and property; processing of loan documentation; closing (paying) the loan; and servicing (collection and record keeping).

FINANCING STATEMENT — The instrument which is filed in order to give public notice of the security interest and thereby protect the interest of the secured parties in the collateral. (See definition of Security Interest and Secured Party.)

FIRST MORTGAGE — A legal document pledging collateral for a loan (See "mortgage") that has first priority over all other claims against the property except taxes and bonded indebtedness. That mortgage superior to any other.

FIRST TRUST DEED — A legal document pledging collateral for a loan (See "trust deed") that has first priority over all other claims against the property except taxes and bonded indebtedness. That trust deed superior to any other.

FISCAL CONTROLS — Federal tax revenue and expenditure policies used to control the level of economic activity.

FISCAL YEAR — A business or accounting year as distinguished from a calendar year.

FIXITY OF LOCATION — The physical characteristic of real estate that subjects it to the influence of its surroundings.

FIXTURES — Appurtenances attached to the land or improvements, which usually cannot be removed without agreement as they become real property; examples — plumbing fixtures, store fixtures built into the property, etc.

FORECLOSURE — Procedure whereby property pledged as security for a debt is sold to pay the debt in event of default in payments or terms.

FORFEITURE — Loss of money or anything of value, due to failure to perform.

FRANCHISE — A specified privilege awarded by a government or business firm which awards an exclusive dealership.

FRAUD — The intentional and successful employment of any cunning, deception, collusion, or artifice, used to circumvent, cheat or deceive another person whereby that person acts upon it to the loss of property and to legal injury. (Actual Fraud — A deliberate misrepresentation or representation made in reckless disregard of its truth or its falsity, the suppression of truth, a promise made without the intention to perform it, or any other act intended to deceive.)

"FREDDIE MAC" — (See **FEDERAL HOME LOAN MORTGAGE CORPORATION.**)

FREEHOLD ESTATE — An estate of indeterminable duration, e.g., fee simple or life estate.

FRONTAGE — A term used to describe or identify that part of a parcel of land or an improvement on the land which faces a street. The term is also used to refer to the lineal extent of the land or improvement that is parallel to and facing the street, e.g., a 75-foot frontage.

FRONT FOOT — Property measurement for sale or valuation purposes; the property measured by the front linear foot on its street line—each front foot extending the depth of the lot.

FRONT MONEY — The minimum amount of money necessary to initiate a real estate venture, to get the transaction underway.

FROSTLINE — The depth of frost penetration in the soil. Varies in different parts of the country. Footings should be placed below this depth to prevent movement.

FULLY INDEXED NOTE RATE — As related to adjustable rate mortgages, the index value at the time of application plus the gross margin stated in the note.

FUNCTIONAL OBSOLESCENCE — A loss of value due to adverse factors from within the structure which affect the utility of the structure, value and marketability.

FUTURE BENEFITS — The anticipated benefits the present owner will receive from the property in the future.

GABLE ROOF — A pitched roof with sloping sides.

GAIN — A profit, benefit, or value increase.

GAMBREL ROOF — A curb roof, having a steep lower slope with a flatter upper slope above.

GENERAL LIEN — A lien on all the property of a debtor.

GIFT DEED — A deed for which there is no consideration.

GOODWILL — An intangible but salable asset of a business derived from the expectation of continued public patronage.

GOVERNMENT NATIONAL MORTGAGE ASSOCIATION — An agency of HUD, which functions in the secondary mortgage market, primarily in social housing programs. Commonly called by the acronymic nickname "Ginnie Mae" (GNMA).

GOVERNMENT SURVEY — A method of specifying the location of parcel of land using prime meridians, base lines, standard parallels, guide meridians, townships and sections.

GRADE — Ground level at the foundation.

GRADUATED LEASE — Lease which provides for a varying rental rate, often based upon future determination; sometimes rent is based upon result of periodical appraisals; used largely in long-term leases.

GRADUATED PAYMENT MORTGAGE — Providing for partially deferred payments of principal at start of loan. (There are a variety of plans.) Usually after the first five years of the loan term the principal and interest payment are substantially higher, to make up principal portion of payments lost at the beginning of the loan. (See Variable Interest Rate.)

GRANT — A technical legal term in a deed of conveyance bestowing an interest in real property on another. The words "convey" and "transfer" have the same effect.

GRANT DEED — A limited warranty deed using the word "grant" or like words that assures a grantee that the grantor has not already conveyed the land to another and that the estate is free from encumbrances placed by the grantor.

GRANTEE — A person to whom a grant is made.

GRANTOR — A person who transfers his or her interest in property to another by grant.

GRATUITOUS AGENT — A person not paid by the principal for services on behalf of the principal, who cannot be forced to act as an agent, but who becomes bound to act in good faith and obey a principal's instructions once he or she undertakes to act as an agent.

GRID — A chart used in rating the borrower risk, property and the neighborhood.

GROSS INCOME — Total income from property before any expenses are deducted.

GROSS MARGIN — With regard to an adjustable rate mortgage, an amount expressed as percentage points, stated in the note which is added to the current index value on the rate adjustment date to establish the new note rate.

GROSS NATIONAL PRODUCT (GNP) — The total value of all goods and services produced in an economy during a given period of time.

GROSS RATE — A method of collecting interest by adding total interest to the principal of the loan at the outset of the term.

GROSS RENT MULTIPLIER — A number which, times the gross income of a property, produces an estimate of value of the property. Example — The gross income from an unfurnished apartment building is $200,000 per annum. If an appraiser uses a gross multiplier of 7%, then it is said that based on the gross multiplier the value of the building is $1,400,000.

GROUND LEASE — An agreement for the use of the land only, sometimes secured by improvements placed on the land by the user.

GROUND RENT — Earnings of improved property credited to earnings of the ground itself after allowance is made for earnings of improvements; often termed economic rent.

HABENDUM CLAUSE — The "to have and to hold" clause which may be found in a deed.

HEIR — One who inherits property at the death of the owner of the land, if the owner has died without a will.

HIGHEST AND BEST USE — An appraisal phrase meaning that use which at the time of an appraisal is most likely to produce the greatest net return to the land and/or buildings over a given period of time; that use which will produce the greatest amount of amenities or profit. This is the starting point for appraisal.

HIP ROOF — A pitched roof with sloping sides and ends.

HOLDER IN DUE COURSE — One who has taken a note, check or bill of exchange in due course: 1. before it was overdue; 2. in good faith and for value; and 3. without knowledge that it has been previously dishonored and without notice of any defect at the time it was negotiated to him or her.

HOLDOVER TENANT — Tenant who remains in possession of leased property after the expiration of the lease term.

HOMESTEAD — (exemption) — A statutory protection of real property used as a home from the claims of certain creditors and judgments up to a specified amount.

HUD — The Department of Housing and Urban Development which is responsible for the implementation and administration of U.S. government housing and urban development programs.

HUNDRED PERCENT LOCATION — A city retail business location which is considered the best available for attracting business.

HYPOTHECATE — To pledge a thing as security without the necessity of giving up possession of it.

IMPERATIVE NECESSITY — Circumstances under which an agent has expanded authority in an emergency, including the power to disobey instructions where it is clearly in the interests of the principal and where there is no time to obtain instructions from the principal.

IMPOUNDS — A trust type account established by lenders for the accumulation of borrowers funds to meet periodic payment of taxes, FHA mortgage insurance premiums, and/or future insurance policy premiums, required to protect their security. Impounds are usually collected with the note payment. The combined principal, interest, taxes and insurance payment is commonly termed a PITI payment.

INCOME (CAPITALIZATION) APPROACH — One of the three methods of the appraisal process generally applied to income producing property, and involves a three-step process— (1) find net annual income,

(2) set an appropriate capitalization rate or "present worth" factor, and (3) capitalize the income dividing the net income by the capitalization rate.

INCOMPETENT — One who is mentally incompetent, incapable; any person who, though not insane, is, by reason of old age, disease, weakness of mind, or any other cause, unable, unassisted, to properly manage and take care of self or property and by reason thereof would be likely to be deceived or imposed upon by artful or designing persons.

INCORPOREAL RIGHTS — Nonpossessory rights in real estate, a rising out of ownership, such as rents.

INCREMENT — An increase. Most frequently used to refer to the increase of value of land that accompanies population growth and increasing wealth in the community. The term "unearned increment" is used in this connection since values are supposed to have increased without effort on the part of the owner.

INDEMNITY AGREEMENT — An agreement by the maker of the document to repay the addressee of the agreement up to the limit stated for any loss due to the contingency stated on the agreement.

INDENTURE — A formal written instrument made between two or more persons in different interests, such as a lease.

INDEPENDENT CONTRACTOR — A person who acts for another but who sells final results and whose methods of achieving those results are not subject to the control of another.

INDORSEMENT — The act of signing one's name on the back of a check or note, with or without further qualification.

INITIAL NOTE RATE — With regard to an adjustable rate mortgage, the note rate upon origination. This rate may differ from the fully indexed note rate.

INITIAL RATE DISCOUNT — As applies to an adjustable rate mortgage, the index value at the time of loan application plus the margin less the initial note rate.

INJUNCTION — A writ or order issued under the seal of a court to restrain one or more parties to a suit or proceeding from doing an act which is deemed to be inequitable or unjust in regard to the rights of some other party or parties in the suit or proceeding.

INSTALLMENT NOTE — A note which provides for a series of periodic payments of principal and interest, until amount borrowed is paid in full. This periodic reduction of principal amortizes the loan.

INSTALLMENT REPORTING — A method of reporting capital gains by installments for successive tax years to minimize the impact of the totality of the capital gains tax in the year of the sale.

INSTALLMENT SALES CONTRACT — Commonly called contract of sale or "land contract." Purchase of real estate wherein the purchase price is paid in installments over a long period of time, title is retained by seller, and upon default by buyer (vendee) the payments may be forfeited.

INSTITUTIONAL LENDERS — A financial intermediary or depository, such as a savings and loan association, commercial bank, or life insurance company, which pools money of its depositors and then invests funds in various ways, including trust deed and mortgage loans.

INSTRUMENT — A written legal document; created to effect the rights of the parties, giving formal expression to a legal act or agreement for the purpose of creating, modifying or terminating a right. Real estate lenders' basic instruments are — promissory notes, deeds of trust, mortgages, installment sales contracts, leases, assignments.

INTEREST — A portion, share or right in something. Partial, not complete ownership. The charge in dollars for the use of money for a period of time. In a sense, the "rent" paid for the use of money.

INTEREST EXTRA LOAN — A loan in which a fixed amount of principal is repaid in installments along with interest accrued each period on the amount of the then outstanding principal only.

INTEREST ONLY LOAN — A straight, non-amortizing loan in which the lender receives only interest during the term of the loan and principal is repaid in a lump sum at maturity.

INTEREST RATE — The percentage of a sum of money charged for its use. Rent or charge paid for use of money, expressed as a percentage per month or year of the sum borrowed.

INTERIM LOAN — A short-term, temporary loan used until permanent financing is available, e.g., a construction loan.

INTERMEDIATION — The process of pooling and supplying funds for investment by financial institutions called intermediaries. The process is dependent on individual savers placing their funds with these institutions and foregoing opportunities to directly invest in the investments selected.

INTERPLEADER — A court proceeding initiated by the stakeholder of property who claims no proprietary interest in it for the purpose of deciding who among claimants is legally entitled to the property.

INTERVAL OWNERSHIP — A form of timeshare ownership. (See Timeshare Ownership.)

INTESTATE — A person who dies having made no will, or one which is defective in form, is said to have died intestate, in which case the estate descends to the heirs at law or next of kin.

INVOLUNTARY LIEN — A lien imposed against property without consent of an owner; example — taxes, special assessments, federal income tax liens, etc.

IRREVOCABLE — Incapable of being recalled or revoked, unchangeable.

IRRIGATION DISTRICTS — Quasi-political districts created under special laws to provide for water services to property owners in the district; an operation governed to a great extent by law.

JOINT NOTE — A note signed by two or more persons who have equal liability for payment.

JOINT TENANCY — Undivided ownership of a property interest by two or more persons each of whom has a right to an equal share in the interest and a right of survivorship, i.e., the right to share equally with other surviving joint tenants in the interest of a deceased joint tenant.

JOINT VENTURE — Two or more individuals or firms joining together on a single project as partners.

JUDGMENT — The final determination of a court of competent jurisdiction of a matter presented to it; money judgments provide for the payment of claims presented to the court, or are awarded as damages, etc.

JUDGMENT LIEN — A legal claim on all of the property of a judgment debtor which enables the judgment creditor to have the property sold for payment of the amount of the judgment.

JUNIOR MORTGAGE — A mortgage recorded subsequently to another mortgage on the same property or made subordinate by agreement to a later-recorded mortgage.

JURISDICTION — The authority by which judicial officers take cognizance of and decide causes; the power to hear and determine a cause; the right and power which a judicial officer has to enter upon the inquiry.

LACHES — Delay or negligence in asserting one's legal rights.

LAND — The material of the earth, whatever may be the ingredients of which it is composed, whether soil, rock, or other substance, and includes free or unoccupied space for an indefinite distance upwards as well as downwards.

LAND CONTRACT — A contract used in a sale of real property whereby the seller retains title to the property until all or a prescribed part of the purchase price has been paid. Also commonly called a conditional sales contract, installment sales contract or real property sales contract. (See REAL PROPERTY SALES CONTRACT for statutory definition.)

LAND AND IMPROVEMENT LOAN — A loan obtained by the builder-developer for the purchase of land and to cover expenses for subdividing.

LANDLORD — One who rents his or her property to another. The lessor under a lease.

LATE CHARGE — A charge assessed by a lender against a borrower failing to make loan installment payments when due.

LATER DATE ORDER — The commitment for an owner's title insurance policy issued by a title insurance company which covers the seller's title as of the date of the contract. When the sale closes the purchaser orders the title company to record the deed to purchaser and bring down their examination to cover this later date so as to show purchaser as owner of the property.

LATERAL SUPPORT — The support which the soil of an adjoining owner gives to a neighbor's land.

LEASE — A contract between owner and tenant, setting forth conditions upon which tenant may occupy and use the property and the term of the occupancy. Sometimes used as an alternative to purchasing property outright, as a method of financing right to occupy and use real property.

LEASEHOLD ESTATE — A tenant's right to occupy real estate during the term of the lease. This is a personal property interest.

LEGAL DESCRIPTION — A land description recognized by law; a description by which property can be definitely located by reference to government surveys or approved recorded maps.

LESSEE — One who contracts to rent, occupy, and use property under a lease agreement; a tenant.

LESSOR — An owner who enters into a lease agreement with a tenant; a landlord.

LEVEL-PAYMENT MORTGAGE — A loan on real estate that is paid off by making a series of equal (or

nearly equal) regular payments. Part of the payment is usually interest on the loan and part of it reduces the amount of the unpaid principal balance of the loan. Also sometimes called an "amortized mortgage" or "installment mortgage."

LEVERAGE — The use of debt financing of an investment to maximize the return per dollar of equity invested.

LEVY — To impose a tax.

LIEN — A form of encumbrance which usually makes specific property security for the payment of a debt or discharge of an obligation. Example — judgments, taxes, mortgages, deeds of trust, etc.

LIFE ESTATE — An estate or interest in real property, which is held for the duration of the life of some certain person. It may be limited by the life of the person holding it or by the life of some other person.

LIFE OF LOAN CAP— With regard to an adjustable rate mortgage, a ceiling the note rate cannot exceed over the life of the loan.

LIMITATIONS, STATUTE OF — The commonly used identifying term for various statutes which require that a legal action be commenced within a prescribed time after the accrual of the right to seek legal relief.

LIMITED PARTNERSHIP — A partnership consisting of a general partner or partners and limited partnersin which the general partners manage and control the business affairs of the partnership while limited partners are essentially investors taking no part in the management of the partnership and having no liability for the debts of the partnership in excess of their invested capital.

LINTEL — A horizontal board that supports the load over an opening such as a door or window.

LIQUIDATED DAMAGES — A sum agreed upon by the parties to be full damages if a certain event occurs.

LIQUIDATED DAMAGES CLAUSE — A clause in a contract by which the parties by agreement fix the damages in advance for a breach of the contract.

LIQUIDITY — Holdings in or the ability to convert assets to cash or its equivalent. The ease with which a person is able to pay maturing obligations.

LIS PENDENS — A notice filed or recorded for the purpose of warning all persons that the title or right to the possession of certain real property is in litigation; literally "suit pending;" usually recorded so as to give constructive notice of pending litigation.

LISTING — An employment contract between principal and agent authorizing the agent to perform services for the principal involving the latter's property; listing contracts are entered into for the purpose of securing persons to buy, lease, or rent property. Employment of an agent by a prospective purchaser or lessee to locate property for purchase or lease may be considered a listing.

LIVERY OF SEISIN (SEIZIN) — The appropriate ceremony at common law for transferring the possession of lands by a grantor to a grantee.

LOAN ADMINISTRATION — Also called loan servicing Mortgage bankers not only originate loans, but also "service" them from origination to maturity of the loan through handling of loan payments, delinquencies, impounds, payoffs and releases.

LOAN APPLICATION — The loan application is a source of information on which the lender bases a decision to make the loan; defines the terms of the loan contract, gives the name of the borrower, place of employment, salary, bank accounts, and credit references, and describes the real estate that is to be mortgaged. It also stipulates the amount of loan being applied for and repayment terms.

LOAN CLOSING — When all conditions have been met, the loan officer authorizes the recording of the trust deed or mortgage. The disbursal procedure of funds is similar to the closing of a real estate sales escrow. The borrower can expect to receive less than the amount of the loan, as title, recording, service, and other fees may be withheld, or can expect to deposit the cost of these items into the loan escrow. This process is sometimes called "funding" the loan.

LOAN COMMITMENT — Lender's contractual commitment to make a loan based on the appraisal and underwriting.

LOAN-TO-VALUE RATI0 — The percentage of a property's value that a lender can or may loan to a borrower. For example, if the ratio is 80% this means that a lender may loan 80% of the property's appraised value to a borrower.

MAI — Member of the Appraisal Institute. Designates a person who is a member of the American Institute of Real Estate Appraisers.

MARGIN OF SECURITY — The difference between the amount of the mortgage loan (s) and the appraised value of the property.

MARGINAL LAND — Land which barely pays the cost of working or using.

MARKET DATA APPROACH — One of the three methods in the appraisal process. A means of comparing similar type properties, which have recently sold, to the subject property. Commonly used in comparing residential properties.

MARKET PRICE — The price paid regardless of pressures, motives or intelligence.

MARKET VALUE — The highest price in terms of money which a property will bring in a competitive and open market and under all conditions required for a fair sale, i.e., the buyer and seller acting prudently, knowledgeably and neither affected by undue pressures.

MARKETABLE TITLE — Title which a reasonable purchaser, informed as to the facts and their legal importance and acting with reasonable care, would be willing and ought to accept.

MATERIAL FACT — A fact is material if it is one which the agent should realize would be likely to affect the judgment of the principal in giving his or her consent to the agent to enter into the particular transaction on the specified terms.

MATURITY DATE — The date by which a loan is to be paid in full.

MECHANIC'S LIEN — A lien created by statute which exists against real property in favor of persons who have performed work or furnished materials for the improvement of the real property.

MEDIATION CLAUSE — A clause in a contract requiring mediation in the event of a dispute.

MERIDIANS — Imaginary north-south lines which intersect base lines to form a starting point for the measurement of land.

MESNE PROFITS — Profit from land use accruing between two periods as for example moneys owed to the owner of land by a person who has illegally occupied the land after the owner takes title, but before taking possession.

METES AND BOUNDS — A term used in describing the boundary lines of land, setting forth all the boundary lines together with their terminal points and angles. Metes (length or measurements) and Bounds (boundaries) description is often used when a great deal of accuracy is required.

MILE — 5,280 feet.

MINOR — A person under 18 years of age.

MISPLACED IMPROVEMENTS — Improvements on land which do not conform to the most profitable use of the site.

MISREPRESENTATION — A false or misleading statement or assertion.

MOBILEHOME — a structure transportable in one or more sections, designed and equipped to contain not more than two dwelling units to be used with or without a foundation system.

MODULAR — A system for the construction of dwellings and other improvements to real property through the on-site assembly of component parts (modules) that have been mass produced away from the building site.

MOLDINGS — Usually patterned strips used to provide ornamental variation of outline or contour, such as cornices, bases, window and door jambs.

MONETARY CONTROLS — Federal Reserve tools for regulating the availability of money and credit to influence the level of economic activity, such as adjusting discount rates, reserve requirements, etc.

MONUMENT — A fixed object and point established by surveyors to establish land locations.

MORATORIUM — The temporary suspension, usually by statute, of the enforcement of liability of debt. Temporary suspension of development or utilities connections imposed by local government.

MORTGAGE — An instrument recognized by law by which property is hypothecated to secure the payment of a debt or obligation; a procedure for foreclosure in event of default is established by statute.

MORTGAGE BANKER — A person whose principal business is the originating, financing, closing, selling and servicing of loans secured by real property for institutional lenders on a contractual basis.

MORTGAGE CONTRACTS WITH WARRANTS — Warrants make the mortgage more attractive to the lender by providing both the greater security that goes with a mortgage, and the opportunity of a greater return through the right to buy either stock in the borrower's company or a portion of the income property itself.

MORTGAGE GUARANTY INSURANCE — Insurance against financial loss available to mortgage lenders from private mortgage insurance companies (PMICs).

MORTGAGE INVESTMENT COMPANY — A company or group of private investors that buys mortgages for investment purposes.

MORTGAGE LOAN DISCLOSURE STATEMENT — The statement on a form which is required by law to be furnished by a mortgage loan broker to the prospective borrower of loans of a statutorily-prescribed amount before the borrower becomes obligated to complete the loan.

MORTGAGEE — One to whom a mortgagor gives a mortgage to secure a loan or performance of an obligation; a lender or creditor. (See definition of secured party.)

MORTGAGOR — One who gives a mortgage on his or her property to secure a loan or assure performance of an obligation; a borrower.

MULTIPLE LISTING — A listing, usually an exclusive right to sell, taken by a member of an organization composed of real estate brokers, with the provisions that all members will have the opportunity to find an interested buyer; a cooperative listing insuring owner property will receive a wider market exposure.

MULTIPLE LISTING SERVICE — An association of real estate agents providing for a pooling of listings and the sharing of commissions on a specified basis.

MUTUAL SAVINGS BANKS — Financial institutions owned by depositors each of whom has rights to net earnings of the bank in proportion to his or her deposits.

MUTUAL WATER COMPANY — A water company organized by or for water users in a given district with

the object of securing an ample water supply at a reasonable rate; stock is issued to users.

NARRATIVE APPRAISAL — A summary of all factual materials, techniques and appraisal methods used by the appraiser in setting forth his or her value conclusion.

NEGATIVE AMORTIZATION — Occurs when monthly installment payments are insufficient to pay the interest accruing on the principal balance, so that the unpaid interest must be added to the principal due.

NEGOTIABLE — Capable of being negotiated, assignable or transferable in the ordinary course of business.

NET INCOME — The money remaining after expenses are deducted from income; the profit.

NET LEASE — A lease requiring a lessee to pay charges against the property such as taxes, insurance and maintenance costs in addition to rental payments.

NET LISTING — A listing which provides that the agent may retain as compensation for agent's services all sums received over and above a net price to the owner.

NOMINAL INTEREST RATES — The percentage of interest that is stated in loan documents.

NONCONFORMING USE — A property use that doesn't' conform to current zoning requirements, but is allowed because the property was being used in that way before the present zoning ordinance was enacted.

NOTARY PUBLIC — An appointed officer with authority to take the acknowledgment of persons executing documents, sign the certificate, and affix official seal.

NOTE — A signed written instrument acknowledging a debt and promising payment, according to the specified terms and conditions. A promissory note.

NOTE RATE — This rate determines the amount of interest charged on an annual basis to the borrower. Also called the "accrual rate", "contract rate" or "coupon rate."

NOTICE — (1) Actual Notice - Express or implied knowledge of a fact. (2) Constructive notice - A fact, imputed to a person by law, which should have been discovered because of the person's actual notice of circumstances and the inquiry that a prudent person would have been expected to make. (3) Legal Notice—Information required to be given by law.

NOTICE OF NONRESPONSIBILITY — A notice provided by law designed to relieve property owner from responsibility for the cost of unauthorized work done on the property or materials furnished therefor; notice must be verified, recorded and posted.

NOTICE TO QUIT — A notice to a tenant to vacate rented property.

NOVATION — The substitution or exchange of a new obligation or contract for an old one by the mutual agreement of the parties.

NULL AND VOID — Of no legal validity or effect.

OBSOLESCENCE — Loss in value due to reduced desirability and usefulness of a structure because its design and construction become obsolete; loss because of becoming old-fashioned and not in keeping with modern needs, with consequent loss of income. May be functional or economic.

OFFER TO PURCHASE — The proposal made to an owner of property by a potential buyer to purchase the property under stated terms.

OFFSET STATEMENT — Statement by owner of property or owner of lien against property setting forth the present status of liens against said property.

OPEN-END MORTGAGE — A mortgage containing a clause which permits the mortgagor to borrow additional money after the loan has been reduced without rewriting the mortgage.

OPEN HOUSING LAW — Congress passed a law in April 1968 which prohibits discrimination in the sale of real estate because of race, color, or religion of buyers.

OPEN LISTING — An authorization given by a property owner to a real estate agent wherein said agent is given the nonexclusive right to secure a purchaser; open listings may be given to any number of agents without liability to compensate any except the one who first secures a buyer ready, willing and able to meet the terms of the listing, or secures the acceptance by the seller of a satisfactory offer.

OPINION OF TITLE — An attorney's written evaluation of the condition of the title to a parcel of land after examination of the abstract of title.

OPTION — A right given for a consideration to purchase or lease a property upon specified terms within a specified time, without obligating the party who receives the right to exercise the right.

ORAL CONTRACT — A verbal agreement; one which is not reduced to writing.

ORIENTATION — Placing a structure on its lot with regard to its exposure to the rays of the sun, prevailing winds, privacy from the street and protection from outside noises.

OSTENSIBLE AUTHORITY — That authority which a third person reasonably believes an agent possesses because of the acts or omissions of the principal.

OVERIMPROVEMENT — An improvement which is not the highest and best use for the site on which it is placed by reason of excess size or cost.

OWNERSHIP — The right of one or more persons to possess and use property to the exclusion of all others. A collection of rights to the use and enjoyment of property.

PACKAGE MORTGAGE — A type of mortgage used in home financing covering real property, improvements, and movable equipment/appliances.

PARAMOUNT TITLE — Title which is superior or foremost to all others.

PARTICIPATION — Sharing of an interest in a property by a lender. In addition to base interest on mortgage loans on income properties, a percentage of gross income is required, sometimes predicated on certain conditions being fulfilled, such as a minimum occupancy or percentage of net income after expenses, debt service and taxes. Also called equity participation or revenue sharing.

PARTIES (PARTY) — Those entities taking part in a transaction as a principal, e.g., seller, buyer, or lender in a real estate transaction.

PARTITION — A division of real or personal property or the proceeds therefrom among co-owners.

PARTITION ACTION — Court proceedings by which co-owners seek to sever their joint ownership.

PARTNERSHIP — A partnership as between partners themselves may be defined to be a contract of two or more persons to unite their property, labor or skill, or some of them, in prosecution of some joint or lawful business, and to share the profits in certain proportions." A voluntary association of two or more persons to carry on a business or venture on terms of mutual participation in profits and losses.

PARTY WALL — A wall erected on the line between two adjoining properties, which are under different ownership, for the use of both properties.

PAR VALUE — Market value, nominal value.

PATENT — Conveyance of title to government land.

PAYMENT ADJUSTMENT DATE — With regard to an adjustable rate mortgage, the date the borrower's monthly principal and interest payment may change.

PAYMENT CAP — With regard to an adjustable rate mortgage, this limits the amount of increase in the borrower's monthly principal and interest at the payment adjustment date, if the principal and interest increase called for by the interest rate increase exceeds the payment cap percentage. This limitation is often at the borrower's option and may result in negative amortization.

PAYMENT RATE — With respect to an adjustable rate mortgage, the rate at which the borrower repays the loan—reflects buydowns or payment caps.

PENALTY — An extra payment or charge required of the borrower for deviating from the terms of the original loan agreement. Usually levied for being late in making regular payment or for paying off the loan before it is due, known as "late charges" and "prepayment penalties."

PERCENTAGE LEASE — Lease on the property, the rental for which is determined by amount of business done by the lessee; usually a percentage of gross receipts from the business with provision for a minimum rental.

PERIMETER HEATING — Baseboard heating, or any system in which the heat registers are located along the outside walls of a room, especially under the windows.

PERIODIC INTEREST RATE CAP — With respect to an adjustable rate mortgage, limits the increase or decrease in the note rate at each rate adjustment, thereby limiting the borrower's payment increase or decrease at the time of adjustment.

PERSONAL PROPERTY — Any property which is not real property.

PHYSICAL DETERIORATION — Impairment of condition. Loss in value brought about by wear and tear, disintegration, use and actions of the elements; termed curable and incurable.

PLAINTIFF — In a court action, the one who sues; the complainant.

PLANNED DEVELOPMENT — A subdivision consisting of separately owned parcels of land together with membership in an association which owns common area. Sometimes the owners of separate interests also have an undivided interest in the common area.

PLANNED UNIT DEVELOPMENT — (PUD) A term sometimes used to describe a planned development. A planning and zoning term describing land not subject to conventional zoning to permit clustering of residences or other characteristics of the project which differ from normal zoning.

PLANNING COMMISSION — An agency of local government charged with planning the development, redevelopment or preservation of an area.

PLAT (of survey) — A map of land made by a surveyor showing the boundaries, buildings, and other improvements.

PLEDGE — The depositing of personal property by a debtor with a creditor as security for a debt or engagement.

PLEDGEE — One who is given a pledge or a security. (See definition of Secured Party.)

PLEDGOR — One who offers a pledge or gives security. (See definition of debtor.)

PLOTTAGE — A term used in appraising to designate the increased value of two or more contiguous lots when they are joined under single ownership and available for use as a larger single lot. Also called assemblage.

PLOTTAGE INCREMENT — The appreciation in unit value created by joining smaller ownerships into one large single ownership.

POINTS — See Discount Points.

POLICE POWER — The right of the State to enact laws and enforce them for the order, safety, health, morals and general welfare of the public.

POWER OF ATTORNEY — A written instrument whereby a principal gives authority to an agent. The agent acting under such a grant is sometimes called an attorney in fact.

POWER OF SALE — The power of a mortgagee or trustee when the instrument so provides to sell the secured property without judicial proceedings if a borrower defaults in payment of the promissory note or otherwise breaches the terms of the mortgage or deed of trust.

PREFABRICATED HOUSE — A house manufactured and sometimes partly assembled before delivery to building site.

PREFERRED STOCK — A class of corporate stock entitled to preferential treatment such as priority in distribution of dividends.

PREPAID ITEMS OF EXPENSE — Prorations of prepaid items of expense which are credited to the seller in the closing escrow statement.

PREPAYMENT — Provision made for loan payments to be larger than those specified in the note.

PREPAYMENT PENALTY — The charge payable to a lender by a borrower under the terms of the loan agreement if the borrower pays off the outstanding principal balance of the loan prior to its maturity.

PRESCRIPTION — The means of acquiring incorporeal interests in land, usually an easement, by immemorial or long continued use. The time is ordinarily the term of the statute of limitations.

PRESUMPTION — An assumption of fact that the law requires to be made from another fact or group of facts found or otherwise established in the section.

PRIMA FACIE — Latin meaning first sight, a fact presumed to be true until disproved.

PRINCIPAL — This term is used to mean the employer of an agent; or the amount of money borrowed, or the amount of the loan. Also, one of the main parties in a real estate transaction, such as a buyer, borrower, seller, lessor.

PRINCIPAL NOTE — The promissory note which is secured by the mortgage or trust deed.

PRIOR LIEN — A lien which is senior or superior to others.

PRIORITY OF LIEN — The order in which liens are given legal precedence or preference.

PRIVATE MORTGAGE INSURANCE — Mortgage guaranty insurance available to conventional lenders on the first, high risk portion of a loan (PMI).

PRIVITY — Mutual relationship to the same rights of property, contractual relationship.

PRIVITY OF CONTRACT — The relationship which exists between the persons who are parties to a contract.

PROCURING CAUSE — That cause originating from a series of events that, without break in continuity, results in the prime object of an agent's employment producing a final buyer; the real estate agent who first procures a ready, willing, and able buyer for the agreed upon price and terms and is entitled to the commission.

PROGRESS PAYMENTS — Scheduled, periodic, and partial payment of construction loan funds to a builder as each construction stage is completed.

PROGRESSION, PRINCIPLE OF — The worth of a lesser valued residence tends to be enhanced by association with higher valued residences in the same area.

PROMISSORY NOTE — Following a loan commitment from the lender, the borrower signs a note, promising to repay the loan under stipulated terms. The promissory note establishes personal liability for its payment. The evidence of the debt.

PROPERTY — Everything capable of being owned and acquired lawfully. The rights of ownership. The right to use, possess, enjoy, and dispose of a thing in every legal way and to exclude everyone else from interfering with these rights. Property is classified into two groups, personal property and real property.

PROPERTY MANAGEMENT — A branch of the real estate business involving the marketing, operation, maintenance and day-to-day financing of rental properties.

PRO RATA — In proportion; according to a certain percentage or proportion of a whole.

PRORATION — Adjustments of interest, taxes, and insurance, etc., on a pro rata basis as of the closing or agreed upon date. Fire insurance is normally paid for three years in advance. If a property is sold during this time, the seller wants a refund on that portion of the advance payment that has not been used at the time the title to the property is transferred. For example, if the property is sold two years later, seller will want to receive 1/3 of the advance premium that was paid. Usually done in escrow by escrow holder at time of closing the transaction.

PRORATION OF TAXES — To divide or prorate the taxes equally or proportionately to time of use, usually between seller and buyer.

PROXIMATE CAUSE — That cause of an event which, in a natural and continuous sequence unbroken by any new cause, produced that event, and without which the event would not have happened. Also, the procuring cause.

PUBLIC RECORDS — Records which by law impart constructive notice of matters relating to land.

PUBLIC TRUSTEE — The county public official whose office has been created by statute to whom title to real property in certain states, e.g., Colorado, is conveyed by Trust Deed for the use and benefit of the beneficiary, who usually is the lender.

PURCHASE AND INSTALLMENT SALEBACK — Involves purchase of the property upon completion of construction and immediate saleback on a long-term installment contract.

PURCHASE OF LAND, LEASEBACK AND LEASEHOLD MORTGAGES — An arrangement whereby land is purchased by the lender and leased back to the developer with a mortgage negotiated on the resulting leasehold of the income property constructed. The lender receives an annual ground rent, plus a percentage of income from the property.

PURCHASE AND LEASEBACK — Involves the purchase of property by buyer and immediate leaseback to seller.

PURCHASE MONEY MORTGAGE OR TRUST DEED — A trust deed or mortgage given as part or all of the purchase consideration for real property. In some states the purchase money mortgage or trust deed loan can be made by a seller who extends credit to the buyer of property or by a third party lender (typically a financial institution) that makes a loan to the buyer of real property for a portion of the purchase price to be paid for the property. In many states there are legal limitations upon mortgagees and trust deed beneficiaries collecting deficiency judgments against the purchase money borrower after the collateral hypothecated under such security instruments has been sold through the foreclosure process. Generally, no deficiency judgment is allowed if the collateral property under the mortgage or trust deed is residential property of four units or less with the debtor occupying the property as a place of residence.

QUANTITY SURVEY — A highly technical process in arriving at cost estimate of new construction and sometimes referred to in the building trade as the "price take-off" method. It involves a detailed estimate of the quantities of raw material (lumber, plaster, brick, cement, etc.,) used as well as the current price of the material and installation costs. These factors are all added together to arrive at the cost of a structure. It is usually used by contractors and experienced estimators.

QUARTER ROUND — A molding that presents a profile of a quarter circle.

QUIET ENJOYMENT — Right of an owner or tenant to the use of the property without interference of possession.

QUIET TITLE — A court action brought to establish title; to remove a cloud on the title.

QUITCLAIM DEED — A deed to relinquish any interest in property which the grantor may have, without any warranty of title or interest.

RADIANT HEATING — A method of heating, usually consisting of coils, or pipes placed in the floor, wall, or ceiling.

RANGE — A strip or column of land six miles wide, determined by a government survey, running in a north-south direction, lying east or west of a principal meridian.

RANGE LINES — A series of government survey lines running north and south at six-mile intervals starting with the principal meridian and forming the east and west boundaries of townships.

RATE ADJUSTMENT DATE — With respect to an adjustable rate mortgage, the date the borrower's note rate may change.

RATIFICATION — The adoption or approval of an act performed on behalf of a person without previous authorization, such as the approval by a principal of previously unauthorized acts of an agent, after the acts have been performed.

READY, WILLING AND ABLE BUYER — One who is fully prepared to enter into the contract, really wants to buy, and unquestionably meets the financing requirements of purchase.

REAL ESTATE — (See Real Property.)

REAL ESTATE BOARD — An organization whose members consist primarily of real estate brokers and salespersons.

REAL ESTATE INVESTMENT TRUST — (See REIT).

REAL ESTATE SETTLEMENT PROCEDURES ACT (RESPA) — A federal law requiring the disclosure to borrowers of settlement (closing) procedures and costs by means of a pamphlet and forms prescribed by the United States Department of Housing and Urban Development.

REAL ESTATE SYNDICATE — An organization of investors usually in the form of a limited partnership who have joined together for the purpose of pooling capital for the acquisition of real property interests.

REAL ESTATE TRUST — A special arrangement under Federal and State law whereby investors may pool funds for investments in real estate and mortgages and yet escape corporation taxes, profits being passed to individual investors who are taxed.

REAL PROPERTY — Land and anything growing on, attached to, or erected on it, excluding anything that may be severed without injury to the land.

REAL PROPERTY SALES CONTRACT — An agreement to convey title to real property upon satisfaction of specified conditions which does not require conveyance within one year of formation of the contract.

RECAPTURE — The process of recovery by an owner of money invested by employing the use of a rate of interest necessary to provide for the return of an investment; not to be confused with interest rate, which is a rate of return on an investment.

RECONVEYANCE — The transfer of the title of land from one person to the immediate preceding owner. This instrument of transfer is commonly used to transfer the legal title from the trustee to the trustor (borrower) after a trust deed debt has been paid in full.

RECORDING — The process of placing a document on file with a designated public official for public notice. This public official is usually a county officer known as the County Recorder who designates the fact that a document has been presented for recording by placing a recording stamp upon it indicating the time of day and the date when it was officially placed on file. Documents filed with the Recorder are considered to be placed on open notice to the general public of that county. Claims against property usually are given a priority on the basis of the time and the date they are recorded with the most preferred claim going to the earliest one recorded and the next claim going to the next earliest one recorded, and so on. This type of notice is called "constructive notice" or "legal notice".

REDEEM — To buy back; repurchase; recover.

REDEMPTION — Buying back one's property after a judicial sale.

REDLINING — An illegal lending policy of denying real estate loans on properties in older, changing urban areas, usually with large minority populations, because of alleged higher lending risks without due consideration being given by the lending institution to the credit worthiness of the individual loan applicant.

REFINANCING — The paying-off of an existing obligation and assuming a new obligation in its place. To finance anew, or extend or renew existing financing.

REFORMATION — An action to correct a mistake in a deed or other document.

REHABILITATION — The restoration of a property to satisfactory condition without drastically changing the plan, form or style of architecture.

REIT — A Real Estate Investment Trust is a business trust which deals principally with interest in land—generally organized to conform to the Internal Revenue Code.

RELEASE CLAUSE — A stipulation that upon the payment of a specific sum of money to the holder of a trust deed or mortgage, the lien of the instrument as to a specifically described lot or area shall be removed from the blanket lien on the whole area involved.

RELEASE DEED — An instrument executed by the mortgagee or the trustee reconveying to the mortgagor or trustor the real estate which secured the loan after the debt has been paid in full.

REMAINDER — An estate which takes effect after the termination of the prior estate, such as a life estate. A future possessory interest in real estate.

REMAINDER DEPRECIATION — The possible future loss in value of an improvement to real property.

RENEGOTIABLE RATE MORTGAGE — A loan secured by a long term mortgage which provides for renegotiation, at pre-determined intervals, of the interest rate (for a maximum variation of five percent over the life of the mortgage.)

RENUNCIATION — When someone who has been granted something or has accepted something later gives it up or rejects it; as when an agent withdraws from the agency relationship.

REPLACEMENT COST — The cost to replace a structure with one having utility equivalent to that being appraised, but constructed with modern materials and according to current standards, design and layout.

REPRODUCTION COST — The cost of replacing the subject improvement with one that is the exact replica, having the same quality of workmanship, design and layout, or cost to duplicate an asset.

RESCISSION — The cancellation of a contract and restoration of the parties to the same position they held before the contract was entered into.

RESCISSION OF CONTRACT — The abrogation or annulling of contract; the revocation or repealing of contract by mutual consent by parties to the contract, or for cause by either party to the contract.

RESERVATION — A right retained by a grantor in conveying property.

RESERVES — 1) In a common interest subdivisions, an accumulation of funds collected from owners for future replacement and major maintenance of the common area and facilities. 2) With regard to mortgage loans, an accumulation of funds, collected by the lender from the borrower as part of each monthly mortgage payment, an amount allocated to pay property taxes and insurance when they are due.

RESPA — (See Real Estate Settlement Procedures Act.)

RESTRICTION — A limitation on the use of real property. Property restrictions fall into two general

classifications—public and private. Zoning ordinances are examples of the former type. Restrictions may be created by private owners, typically by appropriate clauses in deeds, or in agreements, or in general plans of entire subdivisions. Usually they assume the form of a covenant, or promise to do or not to do a certain thing.

RETROSPECTIVE VALUE — The value of the property as of a previous date.

RETURN — Profit from an investment; the yield.

REVERSION — The right to future possession or enjoyment by a person, or the person's heirs, creating the preceding estate. (For example, at the end of a lease.)

REVERSIONARY INTEREST — The interest which a person has in lands or other property, upon the termination of the preceding estate. A future interest.

REVOCATION — When someone who granted or offered something withdraws it; as when a principal withdraws the authority granted to the agent, an offeror withdraws the offer or the Dept of State cancels a salesperson or broker license.

RIGHT OF SURVIVORSHIP — The right of a surviving tenant or tenants to succeed to the entire interest of the deceased tenant; the distinguishing feature of a joint tenancy.

RIGHT OF WAY — A privilege operating as an easement upon land, whereby the owner does by grant, or by agreement, give to another the right to pass over owner's land, to construct a roadway, or use as a roadway, a specific part of the land; or the right to construct through and over the land, telephone, telegraph, or electric power lines; or the right to place underground water mains, gas mains, or sewer mains.

RIGHT, TITLE AND INTEREST — A term used in deeds to denote that the grantor is conveying all of that to which grantor held claim.

RIPARIAN RIGHTS — The right of a landowner whose land borders on a stream or watercourse to use and enjoy the water which is adjacent to or flows over the owner's land provided such use does not injure other riparian owners.

RISK ANALYSIS — A study made, usually by a lender, of the various factors that might affect the repayment of a loan.

RISK RATING — A process used by the lender to decide on the soundness of making a loan and to reduce all the various factors affecting the repayment of the loan to a qualified rating of some kind.

SALE AND LEASEBACK — A financial arrangement where at the time of sale the seller retains occupancy by concurrently agreeing to lease the property from the purchaser. The seller receives cash while the buyer is assured a tenant and a fixed return on buyer's investment.

SALE-LEASEBACK-BUY-BACK — A sale and leaseback transaction in which the leaseholder has the option to buy back the original property after a specified period of time.

SALES CONTRACT — A contract by which buyer and seller agree to terms of a sale.

SALVAGE VALUE — In computing depreciation for tax purposes, the reasonably anticipated fair market value of the property at the end of its useful life and must be considered with all but the declining balance methods of depreciation.

SANDWICH LEASE — A leasehold interest which lies between the primary lease and the operating lease.

SASH — Wood or metal frames containing one or more window panes.

SATISFACTION — Discharge of a mortgage or trust deed from the records upon payment of the debt.

SATISFACTION PIECE — An instrument for recording and acknowledging payment of an indebtedness secured by a mortgage.

SCRIBING — Fitting woodwork to an irregular surface.

SEAL — An impression made to attest the execution of an instrument.

SECONDARY FINANCING — A loan secured by a second mortgage or trust deed on real property. These can be third, fourth, fifth, sixth mortgages or trust deeds, on and on ad infinitum.

SECONDARY MARKET — The buying and selling of existing deeds of trust and promissory notes. The primary market is the one in which lenders loan money to borrowers; the secondary market is the one in which the lenders sell their loans to the large secondary marketing agencies (FNMA, FHLMC, and GNMA) or to other investors.

SECTION — Section of land is established by government survey, contains 640 acres and is one mile square.

SECURED PARTY — This is the party having the security interest. Thus the mortgagee, the conditional seller, the pledgee, etc., are all now referred to as the secured party. (Uniform Commercial Code.)

SECURITY AGREEMENT — An agreement between the secured party and the debtor which creates the security interest. (Uniform Commercial Code.)

SECURITY INTEREST — A term designating the interest of the creditor in the property of the debtor in all types of credit transactions. It thus replaces such terms as the following — chattel mortgage; pledge; trust receipt; chattel trust; equipment trust; conditional sale; inventory lien; etc., according to Uniform Commercial Code usage.

SEISIN (SEIZIN) — Possession of real estate by one entitled thereto.

SELLER'S MARKET — The market condition which exists when a seller is in a more commanding position as to price and terms because demand exceeds supply.

SEPARATE PROPERTY — Property owned by a married person in his or her own right outside of the community interest including property acquired by the spouse (1) before marriage, (2) by gift or inheritance, (3) from rents and profits on separate property, and (4) with the proceeds from other separate property.

SEPTIC TANK — An underground tank in which sewage from the house is reduced to liquid by bacterial action and drained off.

SERVICING LOANS — Supervising and administering a loan after it has been made. This involves such things as — collecting the payments, keeping accounting records, computing the interest and principal, foreclosure of defaulted loans, and so on.

SET BACK ORDINANCE — An ordinance requiring improvements built on property to be a specified distance from the property line, street or curb.

SEVERALTY OWNERSHIP — Owned by one person only. Sole ownership.

SHARED APPRECIATION MORTGAGE — A loan having a fixed rate of interest set below the market rate for the term of the loan which also provides for contingent interest to be paid to the lender on a certain percentage of appreciation in the value of the property against which the loan is secured upon transfer or sale of the property or the repayment of the loan.

SHERIFF'S DEED — Deed given by court order in connection with sale of property to satisfy a judgment.

SIMPLE INTEREST — Interest computed on the principal amount of a loan only as distinguished from compound interest.

SINKING FUND — Fund set aside from the income from property which, with accrued interest, will eventually pay for replacement of the improvements.

SLANDER OF TITLE — False and malicious statements disparaging an owner's title to property and resulting in actual pecuniary damage to the owner.

SPECIAL ASSESSMENT — 1) Legal charge against real estate by a public authority to pay cost of public improvements such as street lights, sidewalks, street improvements. 2) In a common interest subdivision, a charge, in addition to the regular assessment, levied by the association against owners in the development, for unanticipated repairs or maintenance on the common area or capital improvement of the common area.

SPECIAL POWER OF ATTORNEY — A written instrument whereby a principal confers limited authority upon an agent to perform certain prescribed acts on behalf of the principal.

SPECIAL WARRANTY DEED — A deed in which the grantor warrants or guarantees the title only against defects arising during grantor's ownership of the property and not against defects existing before the time of grantor's ownership.

SPECIFIC PERFORMANCE — An action to compel performance of an agreement, e.g., sale of land as an alternative to damages or rescission.

SREA — Society of Real Estate Appraisers.

STANDARD DEPTH — Generally the most typical lot depth in the neighborhood.

STANDBY COMMITMENT — The mortgage banker frequently protects a builder by a "standby" agreement, under which banker agrees to make mortgage loans at an agreed price for many months into the future. The builder deposits a "standby fee" with the mortgage banker for this service. Frequently, the mortgage broker protects self by securing a "standby" from a long-term investor for the same period of time, paying a fee for this privilege.

STATUTE OF FRAUDS — A state law, based on an old English statute, requiring certain contracts to be in writing and signed before they will be enforceable at law, e.g.. contracts for the sale of real property, contracts not be performed within one year.

STATUTORY WARRANTY DEED — A short term warranty deed which warrants by inference that the seller is the undisputed owner, has the right to convey the property, and will defend the title if necessary. This type of deed protects the purchaser in that the conveyor covenants to defend all claims against the property. If conveyor fails to do so, the new owner can defend said claims and sue the former owner.

STRAIGHT LINE DEPRECIATION — A method of depreciation under which improvements are depreciated at a constant rate throughout the estimated useful life of the improvement.

STRAIGHT NOTE — A note in which a borrower repays the principal in a lump sum at maturity whileinterest is paid in installments or at maturity.

SUBAGENT — A person upon whom the powers of an agent have been conferred, not by the principal, but by an agent as authorized by the agent's principal.

SUBDIVISION — A legal definition of those divisions of real property for the purpose of sale, lease or financing which are regulated by law.

"SUBJECT TO" A MORTGAGE — When a grantee takes title to real property subject to a mortgage, grantee is not responsible to the holder of the promissory note for the payment of any portion of the amount due. The most that grantee can lose in the event of a foreclosure is grantee's equity in the property. (See also "assumption of mortgage".) In neither case is the original maker of the note released from primary responsibility. If liability is to be assumed, the agreement must so state.

SUBLEASE — A lease given by a lessee.

SUBORDINATE — To make subject to, or junior or inferior to.

SUBORDINATION AGREEMENT — An agreement by the holder of an encumbrance against real property to permit that claim to take an inferior position to other encumbrances against the property.

SUBPOENA — A legal order to cause a witness to appear and give testimony.

SUBROGATION — Replacing one person with another in regard to a legal right or obligation. The substitution of another person in place of the creditor, to whose rights he or she succeeds in relation to the debt. The doctrine is used very often where one person agrees to stand surety for the performance of a contract by another person.

SUBSIDY BUYDOWN — Funds provided usually by the builder or seller to temporarily reduce the borrower's monthly principal and interest payment.

SUBSTITUTION, PRINCIPLE OF — Affirms that the maximum value of a property tends to be set by the cost of acquiring an equally desirable and valuable substitute property, assuming no costly delay is encountered in making the substitution.

SUM OF THE YEARS DIGITS — An accelerated depreciation method.

SUPPLY AND DEMAND, PRINCIPLE OF — In appraising, a valuation principle starting that market value is affected by intersection of supply and demand forces in the market as of the appraisal date.

SURETY — One who guarantees the performance of another — Guarantor.

SURPLUS PRODUCTIVITY, PRINCIPLE OF — The net income that remains after the proper costs of labor, organization and capital have been paid, which surplus is imputable to the land and tends to fix the value thereof.

SURVEY — The process by which a parcel of land is measured and its area is ascertained.

SYNDICATE — A partnership organized for participation in a real estate venture. Partners may be limited or unlimited in their liability. (See real estate syndicate.)

TAKE-OUT LOAN — The loan arranged by the owner or builder developer for a buyer. The construction loan made for construction of the improvements is usually paid in full from the proceeds of this more permanent mortgage loan.

TAX — Enforced charge exacted of persons, corporations and organizations by the government to be used to support government services and programs.

TAX DEED — The deed given to a purchaser at a public sale of land held for nonpayment of taxes. It conveys to the purchaser only such title as the defaulting taxpayer had.

TAX-FREE EXCHANGE — The trade or exchange of one real property for another without the need to pay income taxes on the gain at the time of trade.

TAX SALE — Sale of property after a period of nonpayment of taxes.

TENANCY IN COMMON — Co-ownership of property by two or more persons who each hold an undivided interest, without right of survivorship; interests need not be equal.

TENANT — The party who has legal possession and use of real property belonging to another.

TENANTS BY THE ENTIRETIES — Under certain state laws, ownership of property acquired by a husband and wife during marriage, which property is jointly and equally owned. Upon depth of one spouse it becomes the property of the survivor.

TENTATIVE MAP — The Subdivision Map Act requires sub dividers to submit initially a tentative map of their tract to the local planning commission for study. The approval or disapproval of the planning commission is noted on the map. Thereafter, a final map of the tract embodying any changes requested by the planning commission is required to be filed with the planning commission.

TENURE IN LAND — The mode or manner by which an estate in lands is held. All rights and title rest withowner.

TERMITES — Ant-like insects which feed on wood and are highly destructive to wooden structures.

TERMITE SHIELD — A shield, usually of noncorrodible metal, placed on top of the foundation wall or around pipes to prevent passage of termites.

TESTATOR — One who makes a will.

THIRD PARTY — Persons who are not parties to a contract which affects an interest they have in the object of the contract.

THRESHOLD — A strip of wood or metal beveled on each edge and used above the finished floor under outside doors.

TIDELANDS — Lands that are covered and uncovered by the ebb and flow of the tide.

TIME IS OF THE ESSENCE — A condition of a contract expressing the essential nature of performance of the contract by a party in a specified period of time.

TIME-SHARE ESTATE — A right of occupancy in a time-share project (subdivision) which is coupled with an estate in the real property.

TIME-SHARE PROJECT — A form of subdivision of real property into rights to the recurrent, exclusive use or occupancy of a lot, parcel, unit, or segment of real property, on an annual or some other periodic basis, for a specified period of time.

TIME-SHARE USE — A license or contractual or membership right of occupancy in a timeshare project which is not coupled with an estate in the real property.

TITLE — Indicates "fee" position of lawful ownership and right to property. "Bundle of Rights" possessed by an owner. Combination of all elements constituting proof of ownership.

TITLE INSURANCE — Insurance to protect a real property owner or lender up to a specified amount against certain types of loss, e.g., defective or unmarketable title.

TITLE REPORT — A report which discloses condition of the title, made by a title company preliminary to issuance of title insurance policy.

TITLE THEORY — Mortgage arrangement whereby title to mortgaged real property vests in the lender.Some states give greater protection to mortgage lenders and assume lenders have title interest. Distinguished from Lien Theory States.

TOPOGRAPHY — Nature of the surface of land; topography may be level, rolling, mountainous. Variation in earth's surface.

TORRENS TITLE — System of title records provided by state law

TORT — Any wrongful act (not involving a breach of contract) for which a civil section will lie for the person wronged.

TOWNHOUSE — One of a row of houses usually of the same or similar design with common side walls or with a very narrow space between adjacent side walls.

TOWNSHIP — In the survey of public lands of the United States, a territorial subdivision six miles long, six miles wide and containing 36 sections, each one mile square, located between two range lines and two township lines.

TRADE FIXTURES — Articles of personal property annexed by a business tenant to real property which are necessary to the carrying on of a trade and are removable by the tenant.

TRADE-IN — An increasingly popular method of guaranteeing an owner a minimum amount of cash on sale of owner's present property to permit owner to purchase another. If the property is not sold within a specified time at the listed price, the broker agrees to arrange financing to personally purchase the property at an agreed upon discount.

TRANSFER FEE — A charge made by a lending institution holding or collecting on a real estate mortgage to change its records to reflect a different ownership.

TRUST ACCOUNT — An account separate and apart and physically segregated from broker's own funds, in which broker is required by law to deposit all funds collected for clients.

TRUST DEED — Just as with a mortgage this is a legal document by which a borrower pledges certain real property or collateral as guarantee for the repayment of a loan. However, it differs from the mortgage in a number of important respects. For example, instead of there being two parties to the transaction there are three. There is the borrower who signs the trust deed and who is called the trustor. There is the third, neutral party, to whom trustor deeds the property as security for the payment of the debt, who is called the trustee. And, finally, there is the lender who is called the beneficiary, the one who benefits from the pledge agreement in that in the event of a default the trustee can sell the property and transfer the money obtained atthe sale to lender as payment of the debt.

TRUSTEE — One who holds property in trust for another to secure the performance of an obligation. Third party under a deed of trust.

TRUSTOR — One who borrows money from a trust deed lender, then deeds the real property securing the loan to a trustee to be held as security until trustor has performed the obligation to the lender under terms of a deed of trust.

TRUTH IN LENDING — The name given to the federal statutes and regulations (Regulation Z) which are designed primarily to insure that prospective borrowers and purchasers on credit receive credit cost information before entering into a transaction.

UNDERIMPROVEMENT — An improvement which, because of its deficiency in size or cost, is not the highest and best use of the site.

UNDERWRITING — Insuring something against loss; guaranteeing financially.

UNDUE INFLUENCE — Use of a fiduciary or confidential relationship to obtain a fraudulent or unfair advantage over another's weakness of mind, or distress or necessity.

UNEARNED INCREMENT — An increase in value of real estate due to no effort on the part of the owner; often due to increase in population.

UNIFORM COMMERCIAL CODE — Establishes a unified and comprehensive method for regulation of security transactions in personal property, superseding the existing statutes on chattel mortgages, conditional sales, trust receipts, assignment of accounts receivable and others in this field.

UNIT-IN-PLACE METHOD — The cost of erecting a building by estimating the cost of each component part, i.e., foundations, floors, walls, windows, ceilings, roofs, etc., (including labor and overhead).

URBAN PROPERTY — City property; closely settled property.

USURY — On a loan, claiming a rate of interest greater than that permitted by law.

UTILITIES — Refers to services rendered by public utility companies, such as — water, gas, electricity, telephone.

UTILITY — The ability to give satisfaction and/or excite desire for possession. An element of value.

VACANCY FACTOR — The percentage of a building's space that is not rented over a given period.

VALID — Having force, or binding force; legally sufficient and authorized by law.

VALLEY — The internal angle formed by the junction of two sloping sides of a roof.

VALUATION — Estimated worth or price. Estimation. The act of valuing by appraisal.

VA LOAN — A loan made to qualified veterans for the purchase of real property wherein the Department of Veteran's Affairs guarantees the lender payment of the mortgage.

VALUE — Present worth of future benefits arising out of ownership to typical users/investors.

VARIABLE INTEREST RATE — (VIRs or VMRs, Variable Mortgage Rates.) An interest rate in a real estate loan which by the terms of the note varies upward and downward over the term of the loan depending on money market conditions.

VENDEE — A purchaser; buyer.

VENDOR — A seller.

VENEER — Thin sheets of wood.

VERIFICATION — Sworn statement before a duly qualified officer to correctness of contents of an instrument.

VESTED — Bestowed upon someone; secured by someone, such as title to property.

VOID — To have no force or effect; that which is unenforceable.

VOIDABLE — That which is capable of being adjudged void, but is not void unless action is taken to make it so.

VOLUNTARY LIEN — Any lien placed on property with consent of, or as a result of, the voluntary act of the owner.

WAINSCOTING — Wood lining of an interior wall; lower section of a wall when finished differently from the upper part.

WAIVE — To relinquish, or abandon; to forego a right to enforce or require anything.

WARRANTY OF AUTHORITY — A representation by an agent to third persons that the agent has and is acting within the scope of authority conferred by his or her principal.

WARRANTY DEED — A deed used to convey real property which contains warranties of title and quiet possession, and the grantor thus agrees to defend the premises against the lawful claims of third persons. It is commonly used in many states but in others the grant deed has supplanted it due to the modern practice of securing title insurance policies which have reduced the importance of express and implied warranty in deeds.

WASTE — The destruction, or material alteration of, or injury to premises by a tenant.

WATER TABLE — Distance from surface of ground to a depth at which natural groundwater is found.

WEAR AND TEAR — Depreciation of an asset due to ordinary usage.

WILL — A written, legal declaration of a person expressing his or her desires for the disposition of that person's property after his or her death.

WRAP AROUND MORTGAGE — A financing device whereby a lender assumes payments on existing trust deeds of a borrower and takes from the borrower a junior trust deed with a face value in an amount equal to the amount outstanding on the old trust deeds and the additional amount of money borrowed.

X — An individual who cannot write may execute a legal document by affixing an "X" (his/her mark) where the signature normally goes. Beneath the mark a witness then writes the person's name and signs his or her own name as witness.

YARD — 3 feet.

YIELD — The interest earned by an investor on an investment (or by a bank on the money it has loaned). Also, called return.

YIELD RATE — The yield expressed as a percentage of the total investment. Also, called rate of return.

ZONE — The area set off by the proper authorities for specific use; an area subject to certain restrictions or restraints.

ZONING — Act of city or county authorities specifying type of use to which property may be put in specific areas.

Made in the USA
Middletown, DE
16 September 2019